GREEK AND ROMAN HISTORIANS

It is today widely accepted that we do not get the whole truth from any historian. *Greek and Roman Historians* applies this undoubted fact to ancient historians such as Herodotus, Tacitus and Thucydides. In this enlightening new work, Michael Grant argues that misinformation, even deliberate disinformation, is abundant in their writings.

Greek and Roman Historians suggests new ways of reading and interpreting the ancient historians, in order to maximise their use as source material. Grant demonstrates that the evidence they provide can be augmented by the use of other sources, literary and non-literary alike.

Michael Grant shows how we can find out something about the ancient world, even if it is not exactly what its historians intended us to know. He argues that their work remains our most important source of information, once we have discounted their sometimes inadequate regard for the truth.

This study is an indispensable guide to the sources for all students of ancient history.

Michael Grant is one of the world's greatest writers of ancient history. He has a distinguished academic career, most recently as Vice-Chancellor of Queen's University, Belfast, and has published over fifty books, including *The Antonines* (Routledge 1994).

GREEK AND ROMAN HISTORIANS

Information and Misinformation

Michael Grant

London and New York

First published 1995
by Routledge
11 New Fetter Lane London EC4P 4EE

Reprinted 1997

Simultaneously published in the USA and Canada
by Routledge
29 West 35th Street, New York, NY 10001

© 1995 Michael Grant Publications Limited

Phototypeset in Garamond by
Intype, London

Printed and bound in Great Britain by
Clays Ltd, St Ives plc

British Library Cataloguing in Publication Data
Grant, Michael
Greek and Roman Historians: Information
and Misinformation
I. Title
937.007202

Library of Congress Cataloguing in Publication Data
Grant, Michael
Greek and Roman Historians: Information and Misinformation
Michael Grant
p.   cm.
Includes bibliographical references and index.
1. Greece—Historiography.   2. Rome—Historiography.
3. Historians—Greece—Biography.   4. Historians—Rome—
Biography.
5. History—Methodology. I. Title
DE8.G73   1995
938'.0072—dc20   94–32012

ISBN 0–415–11769–0 (hbk)
ISBN 0–415–11770–4 (pbk)

CONTENTS

CONTENTS

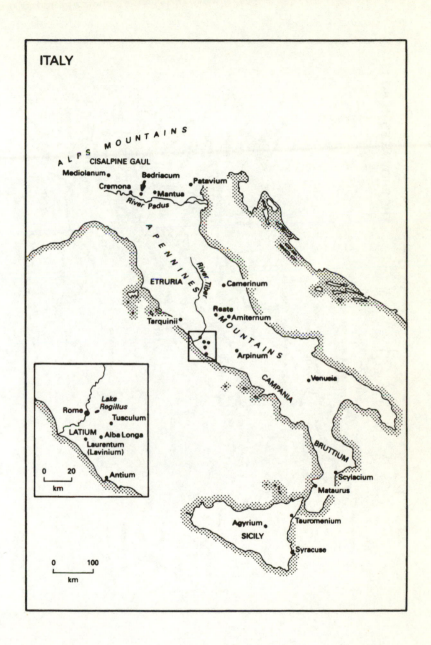

ITALY

ALPS MOUNTAINS

CISALPINE GAUL

Mediolanum

Bedriacum

Patavium

Cremona

Mantua

River Padus

APENNINES

ETRURIA

River Tiber

Camerinum

Reate

Amiternum

Tarquinii

MOUNTAINS

Arpinum

CAMPANIA

Venusia

Lake Regillus

Rome

Tusculum

LATIUM

Alba Longa

Laurentum (Lavinium)

0   20

km

Antium

BRUTTIUM

Scylacium

Mataurus

Agyrium

Tauromenium

SICILY

Syracuse

0   100

km

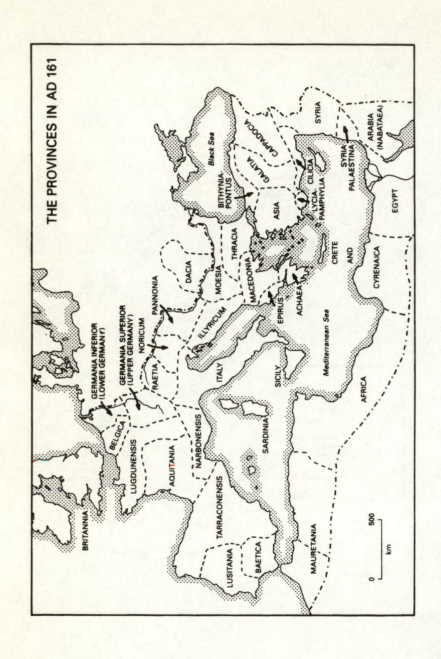

THE PROVINCES IN AD 161

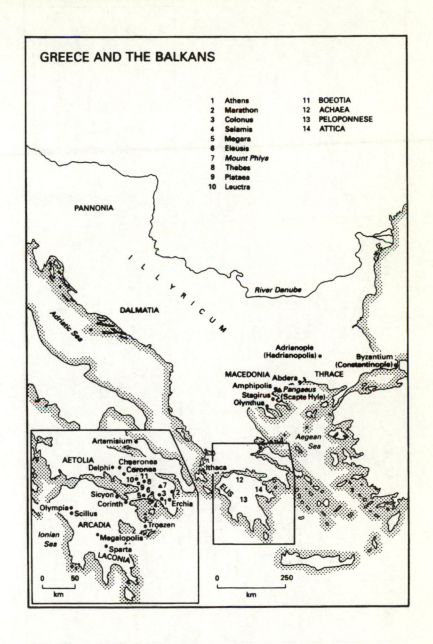

GREECE AND THE BALKANS

1	Athens	11	BOEOTIA
2	Marathon	12	ACHAEA
3	Colonus	13	PELOPONNESE
4	Salamis	14	ATTICA
5	Megara		
6	Eleusis		
7	*Mount Phlya*		
8	Thebes		
9	Plataea		
10	Leuctra		

PANNONIA

I L L Y R I C U M

River Danube

DALMATIA

Adriatic Sea

Adrianople
(Hadrianopolis) •

Byzantium
(Constantinople) •

MACEDONIA   Abdera •   THRACE
Amphipolis • • Pangaeus
Stagirus • (Scapte Hyle)
Olynthus •

*Aegean
Sea*

Artemisium •

AETOLIA
Delphi •   Chaeronea
Coronea
10 • 11
• 8
Sicyon • 9 6 • 7
5 • • 4 • 3 • 2
Corinth   • Erchia

Ithaca

ELIS
12
14
13

Olympia •
• Scillus

ARCADIA
• Troezen

*Ionian
Sea*
• Megalopolis
• Sparta
LACONIA

0   50

km

0   250

km

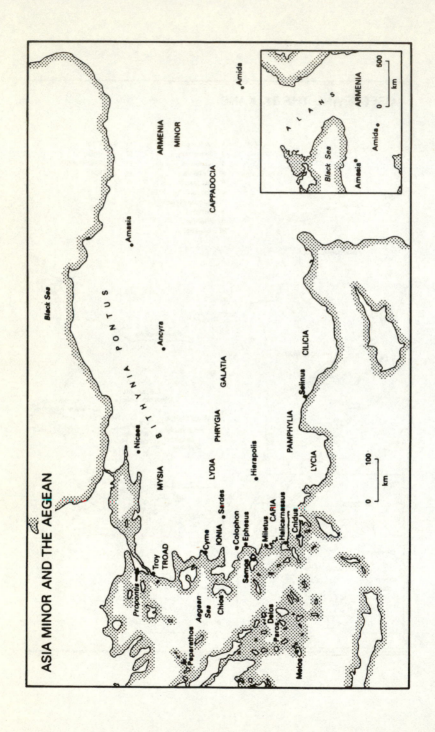

ASIA MINOR AND THE AEGEAN

Black Sea

Amasia

BITHYNIA PONTUS

Ancyra

Nicaea

MYSIA

CAPPADOCIA

ARMENIA MINOR

Amida

GALATIA

PHRYGIA

LYDIA

Sardes

Hierapolis

Troy
TROAD

Cyme

IONIA

Colophon

Ephesus

Miletus

CARIA

Helicarnassus

Cnidus

PAMPHYLIA

Selinus

LYCIA

CILICIA

Proiontis

Peparethos

Aegean
Sea

Chios

Samos

Delos

Paros

Melos

0   100
        km

ARMENIA

ATLAS

Black Sea

Amida

Amasia

0   500
        km

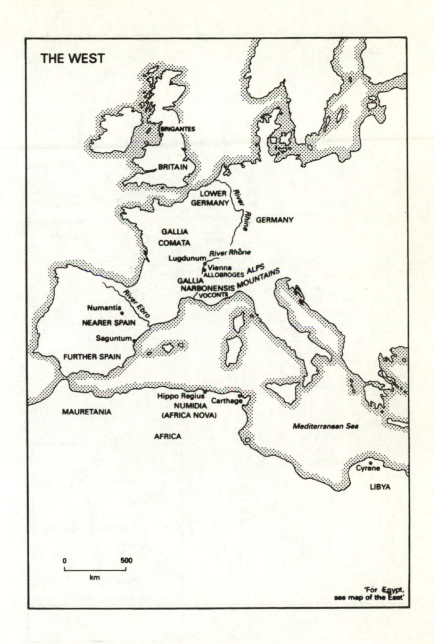

THE WEST

BRIGANTES

BRITAIN

LOWER
GERMANY

River Rhine

GERMANY

GALLIA
COMATA

Lugdunum *River Rhône*

Vienna
ALLOBROGES ALPS
GALLIA MOUNTAINS
NARBONENSIS
VOCONTII

River Ebro

Numantia
NEARER SPAIN

Saguntum

FURTHER SPAIN

MAURETANIA

Hippo Regius
Carthage
NUMIDIA
(AFRICA NOVA)

AFRICA

Mediterranean Sea

Cyrene

LIBYA

0   500
km

'For Egypt,
see map of the East'

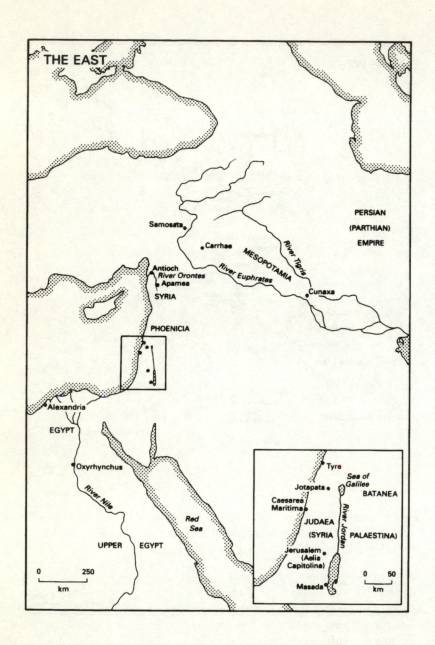

THE EAST

PERSIAN
(PARTHIAN)
EMPIRE

Samosata

Carrhae

MESOPOTAMIA

River Tigris

River Euphrates

Antioch
River Orontes
Apamea

SYRIA

Cunaxa

PHOENICIA

Alexandria

EGYPT

Oxyrhynchus

River Nile

Red
Sea

UPPER   EGYPT

0   250
km

Tyre

Jotapata

Sea of
Galilee

BATANEA

Caesarea
Maritima

JUDAEA
(SYRIA

River Jordan

PALAESTINA)

Jerusalem
(Aelia
Capitolina)

Masada

0   50
km

xii

INTRODUCTION

There are many reasons why we want to know what happened in the Greek and Roman world. I have already set them out in these terms.

> This interest does assume an imperative . . . dimension when it is recalled that we ourselves, whether we like it or not, are the heirs of the Greeks and Romans. In a thousand different ways, they are permanently and indestructibly woven into the fabric of our own existence. . . . Without that massive contribution we should not be what we are. Its influences crowd in upon us insistently from many sides, having reached us in numerous different ways, and at every level of consciousness and profundity.
>
> The Greeks and Romans lived through a variety of events and developments – political, social, literary, artistic – which prefigured and prompted what has subsequently happened, what is still happening, and what will happen in the future, to our own lives and our own communities. Circumstances and backgrounds, of course, have come to differ radically over the centuries. Yet to be able to see no relevant lessons or warnings in this Greco-Roman world would be strangely mistaken. For it is a world that can show us the good and bad things of which humanity has been capable, and may therefore be capable of again . . . . Without awareness of this background we are blindfolded in our efforts to grapple with the future.[1]

But how are we to find out about all of this? Well, first of all there are the Greek and Roman historians. They include some very remarkable writers, and I have written a book trying to point out just how remarkable they were.[2] But I did not, I think, point out sufficiently just how different they were from what we,

1

nowadays, believe that a historian should be: just how different they were, that is to say, from modern historians.

Of course we differ greatly, among ourselves, about what a historian ought to be. This will be considered later, but it can be said here that what we, today, require from a historian is accuracy about the facts together with some accurate, and as far as possible objective, assessment about what the facts signify; in other words, some interpretation of what happened, in the economic and social as well as the political and military spheres.

Chapter 4 of the present book will touch on certain methods and devices utilised by the Greek and Roman historians which are in complete disagreement with these modern requirements. They also used their sources in manners which we find inadequate and surprising (Chapter 3), partly because of their close relationships, much closer than exists today, with other literary genres (Chapter 2). In addition, they lapsed from what we regard as objectivity and accuracy in a variety of fashions. All of this means that the borders between fact and fiction are overstepped in many ways which seem to us inexcusable and which diminish their value as recorders of the events of their times (pp. 90–7).[3]

There was a plethora of ancient historians, but I have regarded it as helpful to restrict my major enquiry to only a few of them. Many of the rest were bad, and a lot of others are little known because their works have wholly or mostly disappeared (pp. 107–18). Since we are trying to discover what is truly characteristic of the most skilful ancient historiography, and how to detect the information and the misinformation that they provide, it seems preferable to concentrate on those of them who are the best, and the best known, and the most likely to be read. This book, therefore, will for the most part deal with Herodotus, Thucydides, Xenophon, Polybius, Caesar, Sallust, Livy, Josephus, Plutarch, Tacitus, Suetonius and Ammianus Marcellinus (ignoring as irrelevant the possible protest that Suetonius and Plutarch are biographers rather than historians).[4]

For the sake of greater completeness, however, another forty historians will be briefly noted and discussed at the end. I feel little regret about having omitted much reference to them from the main part of the book because, first, many of their works are lost and, second, those that are extant mostly reflect to a secondary and inferior degree the qualities that can be seen in the twelve writers whom I have singled out for discussion.

2

Nevertheless, I realise that such a book may invite criticism on the grounds that it is too negative; that is to say, that it devotes most of its attention to pointing out what is wrong even with the twelve Greek and Roman historians whom I have elected to examine. Yet I would not be prepared to accept this criticism, for the following reasons, which I mention briefly here in anticipation of more detailed discussion later on. First, despite all of their deficiencies from our point of view, it is these historians who still provide us with most of the information that we possess about the ancient world: they are our principal source. Yet we cannot make use of them properly unless we acknowledge these very inadequacies. Second, in most cases, they lack nothing in literary quality. Even if they sometimes blur (as we still do today) the barrier between fact and fiction, they write brilliant works of literature (pp. 97–9), and they are enormously worth reading on this account. Third, they deserve careful study precisely because of their very inadequacies. Today we take a somewhat wider view of what history is all about; and we have recourse to further forms of evidence – other literary genres, archaeology, art, inscriptions, coins – to supplement the rather limited evidence that the historians are content to provide for us. I have said something about these additional sorts of evidence in the last two chapters (pointing out that we must be careful about the misinformation that may come to us from these sources as well). Thus, it would not be fair to describe this book as negative. Instead it tries to confront the difficulties of reconstructing the past face to face, and to discover how one ought to proceed.

I should like to offer thanks and acknowledgements to the following for the help that they have given to me: Maria Ellis and John Percival; Jayne Lewin for the maps; and from Routledge: Richard Stoneman, Victoria Peters and Sarah-Jane Woolley. I also warmly appreciate the suggestions that I have received from Rosalind Ramage. I am grateful to the translators whose work I have used and acknowledged, and to Blackwell's who have dealt with queries. And, as on previous occasions, I want to express enormous gratitude to my wife Anne-Sophie, without whom I could not have produced anything at all.

Michael Grant
Gattaiola, 1994

1

ANCIENT AND MODERN HISTORIANS

THE HISTORIANS OF GREECE AND ROME

Historiography in antiquity dealt with important and note-worthy events, or at any rate those regarded as such, according to principles, interests, aims and tastes of great diversity. These events vary according to the social ambience in which a work was composed, according to its intended public, and according to the historiographical tradition to which it belongs .... The different types of history in antiquity aimed at different readers, had different aims, were composed according to different principles.[1]

Herodotus

Herodotus was born in Halicarnassus (now Bodrum) in Caria (south-western Asia Minor) which at the time of his birth (c. 480 BC) was under the rule of the king of Persia. His father, Lyxes, was a member of a distinguished local family, and his uncle, Panyassis, was an epic poet. When, in 461, Panyassis was assassinated by the man in charge of Halicarnassus, who was named Lygdamis, Herodotus abandoned the place, moving to the island of Samos. It is possible that, when Lygdamis later met his end (c. 454?), and Halicarnassus joined the Delian League which was under the control of the Athenians, Herodotus went back to Halicarnassus. If he did, his stay there was brief, since he travelled very widely. It appears probable that in many of the cities and towns that he visited he gave lectures and recitations.

One of these cities was Athens, where he received ample

remuneration for his public appearances. The active part he played in the intellectual life of the place had a large effect on his writings. Nevertheless, before long he continued his journeys, becoming a member of Athens's Panhellenic settlement at Thurii in south-east Italy in 443. Thereafter, he may well have resumed his travels. But it was seemingly at Thurii that he died, in *c.* 425. Subsequently, its peoples displayed his tomb and epitaph to visitors.

The *History* in Greek written by Herodotus and probably designed, at first, to be read aloud (so that he was attentive to his listening public)[2] contained two principal portions. The first tells of the beginnings of the longstanding strife between west and east, the origin and extension of the Persian empire, and the historical background of Greek lands, with particular reference to Athens and Sparta. The second and longer part of the *History* deals with the Persian Wars: the invasions of Greece in 490 BC by Darius I, culminating and terminating in the battle of Marathon, and the invasion of the country ten years later by Xerxes I, signalised by the battles of Thermopylae, Artemisium, Salamis, and finally Plataea (479).

Herodotus believed that these invasions, and the Wars that they caused, were the most significant happenings in the history of the world. As we have seen, however, he envisaged them against a much wider survey, which was nothing less than a general historical picture of the Greek world from the mid-sixth century onwards. That was not presented directly, but through the indirect medium of a vast amount of information which, with unique and extreme ingenuity, displayed by the author's roles as explorer, observer and listener, mirrored the varied multiplicity of what was going on. Most of Herodotus's immense store of information appears to have been gathered before 443 BC, but his work also contains allusions to the early phases of the Peloponnesian War between Athens and Sparta (431–404).

In spite of the faulty character of some of his sources,[3] Herodotus managed to achieve the remarkable feat of creating not only Greek prose – which he wrote in a simple, clear and graceful yet artful style – but also something like a chronological sequence in his vast enquiry. Yet, at the same time, his unfailing, unflagging spirit of enquiry prompted an endless succession of spicy, wonder-loving anecdotes which make him the outstanding entertainer among Greek and Roman historians. This is a reputation which he owes, as R. W. Macan declared, to his inexhaustible interest, his insatiable curiosity, his infinite capacity for taking notes, his flair for a good story, his power of sustaining a continuous narrative, his delight in digression, aside and *bon mot* . . . the lightness of his touch, the grace of his language, his glory in human virtue and achievement wherever to be found, and withal the feelings of mortality, the sense of tears, the pathos of man's fate.[4]

It could be added that he was thoughtful and profound, tolerant as well as wide-ranging.

These are great qualities. They may not be enough to make him a really first-class historian in any modern sense of the word,[5] despite his new and broad concept of what this meant,[6] and despite the fact that he has been proclaimed the 'father of history'.[7] But they made him a magnificent writer, and that is what he was – a man, sometimes ironical and humorous, who, despite much ancient and modern criticism, holds a preeminent place in the literature of the world.

Thucydides

Thucydides was probably born between 460 and 455 BC. He was the son of Olorus, who was Athenian although his name was Thracian, and who left him a property in Thrace, at a place named Scapte Hyle. When the Peloponnesian War between Athens and Sparta began in 431 BC, Thucydides was living at Athens, where he caught the disease described as the Great Plague, from which, however, he recovered.

In 424 Thucydides, as a result of election, became one of the ten Athenian generals for the year. He was given the command of the fleet in the northern Aegean, probably because of his links with the Thracian region. He proved unable, however, to prevent the capture of the key Macedonian city of Amphipolis by the Spartan commander Brasidas. Requested to return to Athens, Thucydides underwent a trial there, and was condemned to twenty years of exile. During his banishment he travelled over extensive areas and formed a large number of contacts. After the Athenians had been finally defeated at the end of the Peloponnesian War (404), he was apparently allowed to go back to their city. It is thought that he died *c*. 400, or not long afterwards.

The *History of the Peloponnesian War* written by Thucydides does not deal with the entire period of the war, since it comes to an end in 411. It is, essentially, something new: a contemporary history,[8] although it includes short but noteworthy accounts of the ancient past and the last fifty years (the Pentekontaetea).

However, he does not concern himself with history in general, contemporary or otherwise, but has selected, like Herodotus, a war as his principal subject. He insisted that the Peloponnesian War, not Herodotus's Persian War, had been the most notable warfare in the whole of the world's history. Even if we feel that the actual hostilities hardly justify such a conclusion, it remains true that they 'provided the lethal convulsion which heralded the entire breakdown of the city-state structure and civilization that had been the principal characteristic of classical Greece'.[9]

That is one reason why the *History* of Thucydides, whatever its numerous defects (of which we shall hear more later), is of permanent importance. That importance is enhanced by his determination to make a distinction between the immediate and the more remote, fundamental, causes of the war with which he was dealing. Unlike Herodotus, whose didactic efforts had been only sporadic, Thucydides, at every juncture, intended to be instructive. He was a social scientist who sought, continually, to deduce general, basic principles and eternal verities from particular events and actions, and who aimed, with profound insight, to make knowledge of these past events a useful, prognostic, permanently valid guide to the future.[10] Meanwhile, although it was a war that principally concerned him, his analysis of Greek society at its zenith was careful and unparalleled.

His method is derived from his exceptional intelligence, and this is the second reason why his *History* is permanently significant: because he was the cleverest and most deeply thoughtful of all historians. It is this cerebral quality, coolly seeking to reconcile literature and science, that gives him his uniqueness. It emerges from his psychological studies, which are devoted to the analysis of masses and groups as well as to individuals. His idiosyncratic style, despite variations of tone, degree and pace, retains the bitter, austere gravity, the severity, the rapid sharpness and the ruthless, condensed, brooding astringency which is required by this task.[11] However, despite the many vivid pictures he presents, this style has seemed to many too difficult to be easily readable or enjoyable. Yet by means of it he brought his chosen form of literature to a point of perfection never later exceeded, and his work has been described as marking 'the longest and most decisive step that has ever been taken by a single man towards making history what it is today';[12] since, for all his faults by modern standards, 'he saw more truly, enquired more responsibly, and reported more faithfully, than any other ancient historian'.[13] He was placed at the head of all ancient historians by the Romantic Revolution.

> Greek historiography reached its peak in the fifth century BC with Herodotus and more especially with Thucydides, whose narrative is perhaps the nearest approach to the ideal history of contemporary events the West has yet known. In particular, his survey of causes and effects, his impartiality in securing evidence from both sides, and his rigorous accuracy of detail established scientific standards which one might confidently have expected to be maintained and revered by his successors.[14]

Such expectations, however, were scarcely fulfilled.

Xenophon

Xenophon was born in c. 428 BC. His father was Gryllus, who belonged to a leading Athenian family. The young Xenophon was originally an orator. He fought in the Peloponnesian War, and also became acquainted with, and admired, Socrates. After the war was over, in 403, and after a shortlived oligarchic revolution brought about by the defeat was replaced by the restoration of democracy, he moved away from Athens.

In 401 Proxenus, a friend of his from Boeotia, asked him to join the cause of Cyrus the younger, who had rebelled against his brother King Artaxerxes II Mnemon of Persia. Cyrus was defeated and killed at Cunaxa (Cunish) in Mesopotamia. Xenophon then helped to lead the evacuation of what had been Cyrus's Greek force to Trapezus (Trabzon, in north-eastern Turkey), from where they returned to their homes.

Xenophon and the men under his command then placed themselves at the disposal first of the Thracian king Seuthes and then of the Spartan commanders Thibron and Dercylidas, who were at that juncture fighting the Persians. While he had been away from Athens, however (it was a time when Socrates had been recently executed, and his sympathisers were in disfavour), Xenophon was condemned to banishment by the Athenians, and his estate and property were confiscated. In 396 he joined Agesilaus I, king of Sparta, against the Persian satrap Pharnabazus, and at Coronea (394) he was allied with the Spartans against his own countrymen. Subsequently he lived in Sparta, and then its rulers gave him a property at Scillus in Elis, in the north-western Peloponnese, where he spent twenty years. In 371, however, after their defeat at Leuctra, the Spartans had to withdraw from the area, and Xenophon and his family moved to the Corinthian Isthmus. In *c.* 365 he seems to have returned to Athens, where his banishment had been revoked. In *c.* 354, at Corinth, he died.

Xenophon wrote the *Hellenica*, a history of Greece from 411 to 362 BC, and the much better, grippingly effective *Anabasis* (*March Up Country*) about his experiences before and after Cunaxa. His *Agesilaus* is a pioneer biographical effort, but too eulogistic, as is also his *Cyropaedia* (*Education of Cyrus*), and his *Constitution of the Lacedaemonians* (Spartans). He also wrote *On Horsemanship*, and his *Hipparchicus*, too, deals with the state cavalry; another of his essays is *On Hunting*. His portrait of Socrates is, of course, interesting, though unreliable, and it is useful to have his views on domestic and national management (*Oeconomicus, Poroi* [*On Ways and Means*, or *On Revenues*])

But even though Xenophon was a versatile man of affairs, his abilities as a historian were distinctly limited and lightweight. Still, he is worth reading not merely because of his simple, intelligible style, but because he engaged so actively, and not unknowledgeably, in those affairs, and because – especially in the *Anabasis* – he had an excellent, exciting story to tell, and told it admirably and vividly: which is a worthy form of literary distinction. He is also worth considering because of his attitudes which mirrored the conflicts of the day: imperialism versus autonomy, Panhellenism versus nationalism, public versus private obligations.

Polybius

Polybius was born at Megalopolis in Arcadia in *c.* 200 BC. His father was Lycortas, a rich landowner who was close to Philopoemen, the leader of the Achaean League. Polybius himself served as a senior cavalry officer (*hipparchos*) of the League, intending to fight on the side of Rome during its Third Macedonian War, against Macedonia's King Perseus. But the Romans (distrusting the League) rejected the force, and after their victory at Pydna (168) deported Polybius and other Achaeans, amounting to a thousand in number, to Italy.

Polybius became tutor to the sons of Lucius Aemilius Paullus, whose younger son Scipio Africanus the younger (Aemilianus) took a liking to him, and enabled him to remain in Rome rather than in an Italian country town. In 151 he left with Scipio for Spain and north Africa, but in the following year he and 300 other deportees were permitted to go back to Greece. After the Third Punic War broke out in 149, he joined Scipio again in Africa, and was present when Carthage was destroyed (146). But the Romans, at this juncture, suppressed the Achaean League and ravaged its capital Corinth, whereupon Polybius was told to reorganise the region, and did so. But he also travelled extensively, and may have witnessed Scipio's capture of rebel Numantia in Spain (133). Some fifteen or more years later, he fell off a horse, and died.

His *Histories* filled forty books, of which the first five have survived intact, and large parts of others are also extant. They are written in a flat style which contrasts sharply with the literary achievements of Herodotus and Thucydides. Or, rather,

> Polybius was not indifferent to style; his care is shown in his scrupulous avoidance of hiatuses .... He did not, as far as we know, follow literary models. To illustrate his dictum and vocabulary we must look not to *belles-lettres* but to the language of officialdom – decrees and dispatches – and technical treatises on philosophy and science .... Polybius was first of all a man of action.[15]

Nevertheless, it must be repeated that Polybius's style is dreary. However, the *Histories* are of outstanding significance, because no other Greek historian has so much to say about historical method, or describes his own attitudes and intentions at such length and with so much care and thought. Polybius's work was epoch-making in the historiography of the Hellenistic age. And he claimed (without any deference to the achievement of Ephorus [pp. 108–9], whose works however are lost) that he was the first to write world history in a systematic manner.[16]

The Hellenistic monarchies were in the end unable to inspire a universal vision of Greek history, which tended increasingly to concentrate on the politics of equilibrium between the great powers. Polybius turned to Rome as the centre of Mediterranean history, following the precocious intuition of Timaeus (p. 110) that what mattered in history was now occurring in the West. This intuition had also been adopted and used by the earliest Roman historians at the end of the third century BC, presenting Rome to the Greek world on the occasion of the clash between Rome and Carthage. It is also worth noting that Polybius added a third element to the polarity between Rome and the Hellenistic monarchies – a third force composed of the Greek federal states.[17]

> Polybius remains the unique expression of the moment in which the Greeks for the first time in their history recognized their complete loss of independence. The Macedonian-Greek symbiosis of previous centuries had not compelled, or even prepared them for, such a catastrophic admission. Polybius was a time-server of genius. . . .
> In the organization of a universal history . . . the plan of his exposition was his own. His own, too, was the emphasis on the practical use of history with which the skilful presentation of Roman history as inevitable and lasting was connected.[18]

Polybius agreed with Thucydides that the only happenings which seem worthy to be recorded are those that are of contemporary or nearly contemporary date, and he emphasised with unremitting didacticism that, like Thucydides, he was presenting a work of practical value, designed to indicate to public figures how they ought, and ought not, to behave. Moreover, it remains true that he 'understood most of the things which a historian should do';[19] though not all of them, by modern standards. But he was quite an innovator, was evidently honest, and he meant to be impartial; he was capable, too, of perceiving essential and epoch-making developments.

Without the writings of Polybius we should know very little indeed about the third and second centuries BC. And what he has given us is a remarkable record of the growth of Roman power. Furthermore, one of his doctrines – that of the 'mixed' constitution which, in his view, was responsible for Rome's success – exercised powerful political influence in the early days of the United States of America. John Adams frequently spoke of him, and it is principally because of Polybius that the constitution of the United States contains the separate powers, limited by a system of balances and checks, which have contributed so largely to its continuing strength.

To the general reader who can find pleasure in seeing an age of transition and vital development through the eyes of a contemporary, who could claim to have lived through stirring events of which he was himself no little part, *quorum pars magna fui*, and who believed that they had a meaning, Polybius's *Histories* remain one of the great books in the Greek language and a splendid point of departure from which to set out in the study of Roman history.[20]

Caesar

Julius Caesar was born in 100 BC. His aunt was Julia, the wife of the leading radical statesman and general Gaius Marius (d. 86). A follower of the latter, Gaius Cornelius Cinna, gave his daughter to Caesar in marriage. After engaging, as a lawyer, in two prosecutions, Caesar proceeded to the island of Rhodes in order to be a pupil of the Greek rhetorician Apollonius Molon. On his way there, he was captured by a gang of pirates, whom he later had crucified. When he returned to Rome, Caesar married again – choosing the granddaughter of Marius's enemy, the dictator Sulla, as his wife.

The rich landowner Crassus backed his political career. In 63 he revived his radical links by attacking the emergency senatorial decree, a conservative institution. He subsequently became chief priest (*pontifex maximus*), governor of Further Spain, and a member (with Pompey and Crassus) of the First Triumvirate (60), gaining the consulship in the following year. Between 58 and 52 he conquered 'free' Gaul (Gallia Comata), beyond the Roman province of southern France (Gallia Narbonensis). This period included also two invasions of Britain (55 and 54).

The death of Crassus at the hands of the Parthians at Carrhae in 53 meant that there were now not three but two prima donnas in the world, Caesar and Pompey; civil war broke out between them, marked by the defeat and death of Pompey (at Pharsalus in 48) and of his elder son Cnaeus (at Munda in 45), with a campaign in north Africa in between these two decisive battles. Caesar was now dictator, but was murdered in 44, on the Ides of March (15 March).

As not only man of action but also literary master, Caesar was astonishingly versatile. His *Gallic War* is the only contemporaneous account of an important Roman foreign war, up to that time, which has survived. The story of the conquest of one of the great European countries, about which we are in consequence better informed than about any other ancient military operation, provides important knowledge about not only the military events but also the various peoples who lived in Gaul at the time. The *Civil War*, in three books, deals with the first two years of that confrontation with the Pompeys, enlarged by narratives of the Alexandrian, African and Spanish wars of 48–45 by officers on Caesar's staff (notably Aulus Hirtius). Although this work, like the *Gallic War*, is intended to present events from Caesar's point of view, it is full of valuable material.

Above all, both writings are composed in a style which is superbly pure, lucid, unadorned, muscular, precise and compressed. Its diction is simple but brilliantly chosen, keeping pace with the rapid movement of events. Such a literary style has won the admiration of subsequent ages.

> Caesar's works, which are the only Commentaries that have come down to us, go far beyond the unambitious tradition of bald, routine accounts. Caesar's style is studied, elegant and spare, an unrhetorical style that is varied and lit up at judicious moments.... It allows the formidable and often ferocious events of the time to speak freshly and urgently for themselves.... His masterly style raises these ostensibly unambitious works far above the level of ordinary Commentary into literary masterpieces that are unmistakably the work of an intellect of exceptional force and power.[21]

Sallust

Sallust (Gaius Sallustius Crispus) belonged to the upper class at Amiternum (San Vittorino), north-east of Rome. Born in *c.* 80 BC, he left for Rome in order to embark on politics. Quaestor in 55 and tribune in 52, he was against the conservatives, and in 50 was one of those removed by the censors from the senate.

When Pompey and Julius Caesar fought against one another, Sallust backed Caesar, who made him quaestor for a second time, thus automatically restoring his membership of the senate. After serving in the army in Illyricum (the former Yugoslavia) and Campania, he participated in Caesar's victory at Thapsus in north Africa (46), and then became the first governor of Africa Nova, the former Numidia (eastern Algeria). After he returned home, however, he was prosecuted for extracting illicit profits from his governorship. Although Caesar ensured that his trial did not take place, he abandoned his public career, withdrawing to the Sallustian Gardens at Rome and other fine estates that he had acquired, until his death in *c.* 35 BC.[22]

Sallust endeavoured to make the best of what had happened to himself by devoting his retirement to the writing of history, which he pronounced to be a continuation of political life. His own experiences were also fitted into the idea that Rome, once so wonderful, had sadly declined. His *Catilinarian War*, telling of the conspiracy of Catiline which was unmasked in 63, reported a decisive stage in this deterioration, and his *Jugurthine War*, about the hostilities against King Jugurtha of Numidia (111–105), described the first challenge by a Roman (Marius) to the supremacy of the governing class. Of the *Histories*, started in *c.* 39 BC, only fragments survive. They dealt with the history of Rome from 78 BC to the early 60s.

Sallust was evidently of the mordant, disillusioned, embittered opinion that all Roman politicians, *populares* and senatorial conservatives alike, were self-seeking, ambitious and insincere: using every situation that arose with ruthless, cynical, aggressively censorious, anti-establishment pessimism and unmitigated revulsion from the present.[23]

His writings, in consequence, though he attempts to make them scholarly and scientific, lack accuracy and objectivity, to such an extent that he is scarcely a historian worthy of the description. Yet his many gifts were outstanding and novel. 'He discovered style and subject congenial to his nature, and he wrought his will on the Latin language, imperiously.'[24] His descriptions were impressionistic, but professional and powerful.

> His [Sallust's] success is partly due to expert organisation of his material. Small incidents are cunningly linked together into units, and each part grows irresistibly to a conclusion – which in turn looks ahead to subsequent events. The supreme example of Sallust's skill is his *Catiline*. Every possible advantage is taken of the striking, tragic theme to create an elegant, close-knit, diversified structure, leading steadily up to a climax. . . . If more of his *Histories* had survived, we should surely have to admire his management of great excit-

ing episodes. They had never been used so extensively in Roman history before, and Sallust must have organised them in clever subordination to a major, sweeping plan, with each book ending on a powerful climactic note.[25]

Against the bland amplitude of Cicero, he recalls the severe abruptness of Thucydides, striving after archaic, pithy, abrasive, epigrammatic effects and abhorring balance and harmony. Despite occasional excess and obscurity, he proved brilliant. His belief was that a historian ought to attain both factual accuracy and stylistic distinction. The former he failed to achieve, but his style, though idiosyncratic, was so remarkable that in a world which saw history not only as truth-telling but as a literary category, its vividness won him an extraordinary distinction among later Romans and indeed continued to conquer the world for centuries to come.[26]

'His ingenious but terse syntax keeps his readers' attention alert'.[27] He was 'the first artistic historian of Rome',[28] and was quickly admired.[29]

Livy

Livy (Titus Livius) was born at Patavium (Padua) in Cisalpine Gaul (north Italy) in 64 or 59 BC. In his early years he proceeded to Rome. He spent most of his remaining years writing his *History*, and died at Patavium in AD 7 or 12. His *History* contained no fewer than 142 books. Those that have survived cover the periods 753–243 and 210–167 BC, but 107 books of this vast work are lost, with the exceptions of fragments and extracts and epitomes.[30]

Livy's account of the Second Punic War (218–201 BC) bears striking witness to his unflagging belief in Rome. As to earlier Rome, he himself warns us that his account contains stories which are purely mythological. Indeed, as regards all periods, doubts have been expressed about whether Livy should not be considered a novelist rather than a historian,[31] because of the psychological interpretations and highly charged scenes of desperation and conflict, like flashes of lightning, which are his speciality.

Yet his narrative, drawing lessons from the past, gives us a wonderful, though over-patriotic, picture of a great nation throughout its history, with all its glories, merits and vicissitudes.[32] 'He was the only historian to have composed a full-length, full-scale history of the growth and expansion of Rome', covering 744 years and eloquently showing how the Romans thought about the past centuries that had witnessed and created the growth of their power.

Livy writes in an attractive flowing style which abandons Sallust's pointed abruptness in favour of the bland rotundity of Cicero. This is the 'milky abundance' which Quintilian ascribed to him, a broad, urbane, ornate, orderly richness.[33] Furthermore, his story was flexibly and dramatically structured.

> Noteworthy first is the artistic skill which lies behind the general organisation of the material: the *Ab Urbe Condita* is carefully divided into *pentads*. . . . Each *pentad* has a compositional unity. . . . Livy found much of this already in his sources. He has merely to add the necessary information, and then concentrate on enhanced literary effects.[34]

This first-rate literary excellence ensured Livy an enormous and immediate success, eclipsing all forerunners and rivals, and providing Europe with its principal information (even if not always accurate) about how the Romans might be supposed to have acted and thought, and how they achieved their massive successes. 'So far as enthusiasm serves . . . Livy penetrates to the spirit of ancient times.'[35]

Josephus

Josephus, born in AD 37–38, was a Jew, the son of Matatyahu (Matthias), who belonged to the elevated priestly class, and of a woman who was related to the former Hasmonaean (Maccabee) royal family. The first language of Josephus was Aramaic, but he was educated in Hebrew, and he wrote in Greek. During his youth he successively became an adherent of all the three main branches of Judaism – the Sadducees, Essenes and Pharisees – and remained with the last-named, becoming a priest. In *c.* 64 he went to Rome in order to defend a colleague who had been arrested there, and with the help of a Jewish actor, Aliturus, and of the emperor's wife Poppaea Sabina, he undertook this task successfully.

When he returned to Judaea, the First Jewish Revolt (First Roman War) was about to break out. Josephus was not hopeful about its chances. Nevertheless, when the rebellion was launched in AD 66, the current Jewish leaders (of moderate inclinations) dispatched him to take command of their force in Galilee. When Vespasian, the Roman governor of Syria, came near with his army, Josephus retired to Jotapata, where, after a seven-month siege, he evaded a Jewish suicide pact and went over to the Romans. After keeping him under arrest for a time, they let him go, and during the subsequent siege of Jerusalem he acted as the interpreter of the Roman commander-in-chief, Vespasian's son Titus. After the Romans had captured the city, he went with Titus first to Alexandria and then to Rome, where he was given a pension and Roman citizenship. He adopted the name Flavius, which was that of Vespasian and Titus, and accepted Vespasian's recommendation about the woman he should marry, the first of his three Jewish wives.

Josephus was the most important Jewish historian.[36] At Rome he wrote his *History of the Jewish War*. If it were not for his work we should know little about the war. Although biased and inaccurate in a number of respects, Josephus displayed great technical skill in the construction of his work, in which he brought home, and made intelligible, the tension, religious fanaticism, brutality and horrors which characterised this series of events: for example, his description of the siege and mass suicide at Masada is unforgettable.

Subsequently, he wrote a more comprehensive history of his people, the *Jewish Antiquities* (*Archaeologia*). Although Josephus's knowledge of his own religion is unprofound and at times inaccurate, and although he has to be at pains not to upset Roman opinions, his work constitutes a remarkable and highly individual praise of Jewry and assessment of Judaism in the first century AD. The Christians, too, saw his long and grim account of the destruction of Jerusalem in his *Jewish War* as a fulfilment of New Testament prophecies.

St Jerome not unjustifiably called him 'the Greek Livy'.[37]

Plutarch

Plutarch was born before AD 50 at Chaeronea in Boeotia (central Greece), where he was a member of one of the principal local families and spent most of his life, although he also went to Athens and travelled to other places as well, including Rome, where he was sent on a political mission. Plutarch became a Roman citizen, and adopted the family name of Lucius Mestrius Florus (consul in AD 72), whom he accompanied on a visit to Bedriacum, between Cremona and Mantua, the site of the two most important battles during the Civil Wars of AD 69.

While at Rome, Plutarch gave lectures, in Greek, on philosophical and rhetorical topics, and in the early 90s, a famous man, he visited Rome and lectured again. He also travelled in the near east, receiving numerous honours.

Widely read, and the possessor of a well-stocked memory, he wrote, in Greek, a huge number of works, on a great variety of themes. Reference may be made here to his study *On the Malice of Herodotus* and his *Greek and Roman Enquiries*. By far his best-known writings are his biographies, mostly written between 105 and 115. These are accounts of officers and politicians, many of which are grouped in pairs, one Greek and one Latin. This is, historically, a faulty step to have taken, but it does symbolise the essential feature of the life of Plutarch himself: he was a Greek who, while lacking national bias, was conscious of his Greekness, and by no means ashamed of it, and yet completely accepted the role of the Romans as the dominant power. Unobtrusively, he advocated the coming together of the two cultures.

Something will be said later about the earlier development of biography in connection with Nepos and writers before him (pp. 102–3). As for Plutarch,

> one of his strengths is the inclusion in his biographies of a vast range of actions, sayings and minor peculiarities that seemed to him significant.... His special gift lies in his choice of intimate anecdotes, calculated to catch the attention of his readers and to bring out the moral character of his subjects. He ... gives us the illusion of entering into their hearts and their thoughts, so that famous men are enlivened by day-to-day human incidents, in a spirit of gentleness, friendliness and family feeling. [He displays an] unerring sense of detail, and vivid and memorable narrative, and his flexible and controlled style varies in complexity and richness between the reflecting passages ... and the narrative.[38]

As for his secure place in literature, he is 'a conscious artist in an elaborate manner, meticulous in his periodic structures, his studied word-patterns, his avoidance of hiatus, and his carefully chosen vocabulary'.[39] Plutarch is eminently readable. As Michel de Montaigne observed: 'I cannot easily do without Plutarch. He is so universal and so full that, on every occasion, however extraordinary your subject, he is at hand to your need.' Although Plutarch rarely breaks original ground, he uses the tradition skilfully, quietly imposes his own personality, and provides much information and many ideas.

Tacitus

It seems likely that the family of the writer Publius Cornelius Tacitus were from Cisalpine Gaul (north Italy) or Narbonese Gaul (southern France). His father may have been procurator (representative of the emperor) in Lower Germany and paymaster for the Roman Rhine army.

After studying rhetoric at Rome in *c.* AD 75, subsequently Tacitus became a highly esteemed orator. In 77 he married the daughter of one of the consuls of the year, Cnaeus Julius Agricola. In the same year, or a little earlier, he served as military tribune in a legion, and shortly after Domitian came to the throne (81) he became quaestor, thus entering the senate. Then he moved up to the praetorship (88), but subsequently left for appointments in the provinces. He was in Rome, however, when Domitian persecuted the senate during the last years of his reign. Under Nerva (96–98), Tacitus became consul, and towards the end of Trajan's life he was proconsul of Asia (112–113). Whether he survived to witness the beginnings of Hadrian's reign (117) is disputed.

Tacitus wrote the *Germania* (98), about the peoples of that country, and, in the same year, the *Agricola*, in praise of his father-in-law. After a *Dialogue On Orators* (*c.* 102), he composed his *Histories* (*c.* 109). They dealt with Roman history from 68 to 96, but only the earlier part of the work has survived. The *Annals* (*c.* 117?), about the earlier period beginning in AD 14, are mostly extant.

Although far from fair, Tacitus is a believer in the lofty dignity and nobility of history, and a writer of outstanding excellence, utilising a highly individual and sometimes ironical manner which imposes his personality upon us. The *Histories* constitute an almost incredible *tour de force*.

The whole period of the Civil Wars, uniquely reproduced and reconstructed by Tacitus, is seen as dominated by wild uncontrollable forces and irrational emotions: greed, lust for power, barbarous mob violence, hysteria, the breakdown of all loyalties except to oneself. The overall impression is of the futility of human behaviour.[40]

However, human beings, Tacitus maintained, are capable of great virtue, courage and perseverance.

The *Annals* are more magnificent and acerbic still, full of extraordinary and gripping stories:

a masterly artistic achievement, an achievement very largely the result of his manner of writing. Tacitus wrote in a totally personal, highly individual, knife-edged development of Sallust's anti-Ciceronian style, combined with the Silver Latin 'point' that had been a feature of post-Augustan writing. His vividly abrupt sentences and flashing, dramatic epigrams ... terminate in unexpected, trenchant punch-lines.[41]

Even if, by modern standards, the intense, incisive, sombre, full-toned, staccato, allusive, surprising, suspenseful style of Tacitus seems laboured, even precious, with all of its dislocation and point and insinuation, its swiftness and plausibility and suggestive brevity keeps us constantly on the alert. Words are arranged in arresting, and often violent, order and the views of Tacitus are closely linked with these stylistic peculiarities. He himself admitted, and expected, that his work would be more useful than enjoyable.[42]

Yet 'Tacitus', wrote Thomas Jefferson, 'I consider the first writer in the world without a single exception.' That is true, if we are content to see him as a marvellous literary figure and not necessarily, in the modern sense, as a historian.[43]

Suetonius

Suetonius (Gaius Suetonius Tranquillus) belonged to a family of knightly rank (*equites*) which is likely to have come from Hippo Regius in north Africa (now Annaba in Algeria). Born in c. AD 70, he went to Rome, where he was perhaps a teacher of literature and a lawyer. In c. 110–112 he worked under Pliny the younger when the latter was governor of Bithynia-Pontus (northern Asia Minor). Then Suetonius held various posts at the imperial court in Rome, culminating with the duty of looking after the correspondence of Hadrian. In 122, however, he was reportedly dismissed from that function, because he had been rude to the empress Sabina.

Suetonius was not so much a historian, in the usual sense of the word, as a biographer. In the reign of Trajan (98–117) he wrote, in Latin, *The Lives of Famous Men*, brief sketches of Roman literary figures, of which a few sections have survived, but the portion devoted to historians has vanished, with the exception of a single fragment. Then he composed his famous *Lives of the Caesars* – that is to say, the Twelve Caesars, from Julius Caesar to Domitian – which, apart from one short section, is still extant.

Suetonius apparently felt that the historical writings of Tacitus were too grand to compete with. And he regarded the chronological method of the Greek biographer Plutarch as inappropriate. Instead he adopted a technique – in all likelihood not entirely novel – of varying his narrative accounts by the interspersion of material illustrating the chief characteristics of his biographical subjects. This was a method which made it possible for him to delineate, by minute and laborious effort and research, the personal and sometimes trivial details that historians regarded as beneath their notice, in order to satisfy the curiosity of the public regarding the lives of his characters as ordinary beings. He left it to his readers, however, to add up for themselves a series of disconnected items to see what they amounted to.

Suetonius, although capable of a telling narrative, avoided style and eloquence, writing straightforwardly but in a rather abrupt and staccato way. His principal contribution to biography (and thus to historiography) was the new and relatively advanced degree of indifferent impartiality that he managed to maintain, introducing in his own dry and impressionistic manner information that reflected both well and badly upon the men he was considering.

Pliny the younger described him as *eruditissimus*, most scholarly or learned. This is not really what his writings show him to be. Or, at least, that was not his aim, which was to make it clear, by direct and efficient, though carefully chosen and arranged, writing, that people's personalities are made up of contradictory, uncohesive features. In working towards this aim Suetonius displayed a conspicuous absence of the moralistic factor which, as we shall see elsewhere, had constituted such an important element in earlier Greek and Latin biography. That is why the *Historia Augusta* feels able to name him among those historians and biographers who have written not so much with eloquence as with truthfulness (*non tam diserte quam vere*).[44]

Ammianus Marcellinus

Ammianus Marcellinus (*c*. AD 330–395), although he wrote in Latin, belonged to a prosperous Greek family of Antioch (Antakya) in Syria (now in south-eastern Turkey). It seems likely that he was a member of the 'curial' class, a rich, hereditary element of society with an ancestry provided by city councillors.

During the reign of Constantius II (337–361), the son of Constantine I the Great, Ammianus was an officer of the *protectores domestici*, the imperial household guard. In *c*. 353 he began to serve under Ursicinus, the general in command of the Roman garrison at Nisibis in Mesopotamia (now Nüsaybin in Turkey), situated on the frontier of the Roman empire facing Persia. In 355 he went with Ursicinus to Gaul in order to help to suppress the rebellion of Silvanus. He remained there to participate, in the following year, in the first German campaign of Julian. In 357, however, he was sent back to the eastern frontier, where he took part in warfare against the Persians. In 359 he was shut up in Amida (Diyarbakir, in south-eastern Turkey) which was under siege from the enemy. He escaped, and subsequently joined in the Persian expedition of Julian, who was now emperor ('Julian the Apostate') but who died of wounds in 363. He was succeeded by Jovian, who evacuated the region, and was accompanied by Ammianus to Antioch.

But Jovian, too, died in the following year, and the empire was divided into two parts, eastern and western. After Gratian (the son of Valentinian I) came to the throne in 378, in the western section (with its capital initially at Mediolanum [Milan]), Ammianus took up residence in Rome, where he spent much of the rest of his life. He also travelled a good deal, going back, for a time, to Antioch, in the eastern empire. He died in *c*. 395.

During the latter years of his life Ammianus wrote his long *Roman History*, covering the epoch between the accession of Nerva in AD 96 and the death of the eastern emperor Valens at the battle of Adrianople (Edirne) against the Visigoths in 378. This *History* has been described as 'an astonishing apparition, an original mind in history after centuries of dry rot'. The work's last eighteen books beginning in 353, have survived. They provide, in a style that is too exuberant and hyperbolic to be really attractive, an invaluable, and for the most part accurate, account of what happened during Ammianus's own lifetime.[45] He offers information regarding matters that he knew about from his own personal knowledge and activity, and had absorbed into his original, curious and inquisitive mind. The main significance of the work lies in this information, since it is otherwise a period about which we are inadequately enlightened. Another reason for its significance is the moderation of Ammianus (despite certain partisanships); such a quality was infrequently encountered at the time, or indeed among ancient historians in general.

Ammianus provides subtle assessments, and displays an acute comprehension. But the work is also interesting because of his conviction that the empire, like eternal Rome itself, would last for ever. This view, which was widely held, proved wrong, but Ammianus nevertheless offers a unique picture of this period of cataclysmic change. He is noteworthy too because, despite this pro-Roman attitude, he was a Greek, so that, following along the path delineated by Plutarch, he aptly epitomises the mixture of the two cultures which had constituted the ancient world and which was now about to come to an end.

Ammianus, observed Syme, was an honest man in an age of fraud and mendacity and fanaticism.[46] 'It is not without the most sincere regret', said Edward Gibbon, 'that I must now take leave of an accurate and faithful guide.'[47]

2

THE HISTORIANS AND OTHER DISCIPLINES

HISTORY AND POETRY

Epic Poetry

The debt of the ancient historians to Homer was enormous. For one thing, the Trojan War was regarded as a historical event, and Homer's telling of it was believed to be historically accurate – or not far off it, requiring only a certain amount of rationalisation in order to be converted into history.[1] Everyone accepted the epic tradition as grounded on hard fact,[2] and the Homeric heroes were believed in some sense to be the forebears of the Greeks of later times. The speeches too, which play such a large part in ancient historiography, go back to Homer; so does the conversation, and likewise the story-telling. Of course, since the Greeks included a number of sceptics, not everybody believed in the essential historicity of Homer.[3] Yet, by and large, Greek historiography remained firmly grounded on Homer and the epic.[4]

One result of this was that, although, in the *Iliad*, Achilles denounces deceitful words, Odysseus' lies and false tales of what he had done were rather admired. They were a sign of his famous resourcefulness (*metis*);[5] and literary lying was traced back to him.[6] He is like the trickster figures of folk tales, or like Jacob, the 'Artful Dodger' of the Biblical world, the source of many stories.

Certainly, Stesichorus was notoriously unimpressed by the whole story of Helen, and Xenophanes attacked the credibility of Homer and Hesiod. Later, Eratosthenes too refused to accept the tradition of Homer's omniscience and infallibility.[7] Indeed, Hesiod himself had already been aware that part of his own epic tradition was historically unauthentic: 'We know how to tell many false-

25

hoods that seem real: but we also know how to speak truth when we wish to.'[8] And he himself probably added to the falsehoods, which Plato attributed both to him and to Homer.[9] It was more polite, however, to regard Homer as allegorical.[10]

Hecataeus wrote, 'The stories of the Greeks are many and ludicrous, as they appear to me.'[11] It has been suggested that he was referring not to the epic myths but to genealogical traditions,[12] but it is also probable that, being a rationaliser, he had the Homeric accounts in mind as well. Nevertheless, the influence of Homer upon the framing of Greek histories remained vast.

This is apparent in Herodotus. True, while generally uncomplimentary about Hecataeus, he joined him in criticising old Greek stories, and conscientiously separated the ages of myth and history.[13] But he owed an enormous amount to Homer,[14] seeing the Persian Wars as directly descended from the Trojan War. His dialogues and speeches and digressions are Homeric, and so is his stress on divine epiphanies and army catalogues and leaders' individual valour, with little notice taken of strategic arguments. Homer inspired him, and he was compared to Homer and has even been called the 'Homer of the Persian Wars',[15] while the innumerable fables which this role involved earned him the title of *mythologos*.[16] And he himself, while careful to insist upon the innovative distinction of factual truth from falsehood, was surely content to see himself as a creative heir of the epic tradition.

As for Thucydides, he saw that Herodotus was too mythical, and so he refuted Homer and sought to divorce causation from epic poetry.[17] Yet, all the same, he did not really reject the Homeric tradition, but merely tidied it up and rationalised it, eliminating what he saw as its exaggerations.[18] He remained content however to name Minos and Agamemnon as real persons,[19] creating the early history of Greece out of mythology. By the same token Polybius believed that Odysseus existed, identifying himself with the hero as a great traveller.[20]

When we come to the Romans, we find that Livy, despite his probable awareness of the mythological nature of these stories, is content (motivated in part, he says, by deliberate escapism) to frame the early history of Rome in terms of what were obviously fictitious legends.[21] He also directly echoes the Homeric epic: the encounter between Marcus Valerius and the young Tarquinius is modelled on the duel between Paris and Menelaus,[22] the battle of

Lake Regillus is distinctly Homeric,[23] and Cannae becomes a series of unconnected, Homeric engagements.[24]

Tacitus, too, was affected by the epic tradition, which indeed exercised a powerful formative influence on his work. The burning of Cremona and Rome in the *Histories* owes much to the Homeric burning of Troy,[25] though elsewhere it is Virgil rather than Homer whose poetry is echoed. Thus Tacitus follows Virgil in employing tableaux to evoke a wide range of emotions in the reader, so that the historian, although writing in prose, has been described as 'one of the few great poets of the Roman people'.[26]

Plutarch still regarded Theseus and Romulus as historical figures,[27] and Ammianus Marcellinus repeated the frequent Virgilian echoes of Tacitus. For the Christians, the whole of history became a divine epic.

To sum up,

> The Greeks themselves, and the Romans, knew that there were two differences between history and epic poetry: history was written in prose, and was meant to separate facts from fancies about the past. [But] Homer was too much of an authority not to be used by historians as evidence for specific facts.[28]

Tragic Poetry

The link of historiography with epic shows what a poetical affair ancient history seemed to be; ancient historians often preferred general poetical 'truth' to factual accuracy. They have also had some modern followers, such as Lytton Strachey, who wrote that 'every history worthy of the name is, in its own way, as personal as poetry'; although the purpose of poetry, as Eratosthenes pointed out, is not to instruct but to entertain: and Lucian thought it appropriate to keep the two disciplines apart.[29] In so doing, he was following Aristotle, who wrote:

> The distinction between historian and poet is not in the one writing prose and the other verse – you might put the work of Herodotus into verse, and it would still be a species of history. It consists really in this, that the one describes the thing that has been, and the other a kind of thing that might be. Hence poetry is something more philosophic and of graver import than history, since its statements are of the

nature rather of universals, whereas those of history are singulars.

Nevertheless, it remains inescapably true that ancient historians maintain many links with poets – and should, indeed, be compared to them.

In addition to their epic links, they also owe a tremendous amount to tragedy, which, like their own art, originated from epic and which, often, was by no means remote from contemporary history, as an investigation of the great Athenian tragic poets reveals.[30]

> The official position of the literary genre of tragedy in the cultural and social life of the Athenian *polis* makes it a priori likely that it was related to a particular political situation and had a substantial 'political' character.
>
> The choice of contemporary themes by ... Aeschylus shows clearly the wish of the author to express views of contemporary relevance. ... The fact that Sophocles took an active part in the political life of Athens, even holding office, does not make the historical interpretation of his tragedies any easier. ... The historical use of tragedy is on safer ground when it pursues an understanding of an astonishingly lively milieu, in social, political and cultural terms, and of an age passionately involved in dramatic choices.
>
> These points are even more valid for the tragedies of Euripides, which closely reflect human reality and seem also to follow more closely than other plays the social changes and the shifts in public opinion which accompanied the political situation as it unfolded during the Peloponnesian War.[31]

Herodotus's emphasis on the *nemesis* and *hubris* and *peripeteia* which fall upon eminent people (such as King Croesus of Lydia), at the behest of a jealous god, is powerfully tragic; and his speeches, although an epic feature, probably came to him through the intermediacy of drama. Probably his debt to tragedy, which he passed on to others, was a result of his residence at Athens, where he saw and knew of the contemporary plays that have been mentioned. Fragments have even been discovered of the tragic play on which his fairy-tale of King Gyges was based.[32]

As for Thucydides, he is an extremely dramatic writer – the Melian Dialogue, for example, is in full dramatic form – even if, despite his kinship with Euripides, doubts have been expressed whether contemporary tragedies were among the literary influences that most affected him.[33]

At some stage or other, a sort of 'tragic history' was invented, which deliberately merged the two. The origins of this sort of amalgamation have been much debated – perhaps it was as early as the fifth century BC – and there was not always a very clear-cut distinction between 'tragic' and 'rhetorical' history: both sought to entertain, and serve (supplanting the poets) as popular teachers.[34]

However, Polybius saw quite clearly that there was an essential difference between history and tragedy, and approved of Aristotle's distinction between them:

> A historical author should not try to thrill his readers by such exaggerated pictures, nor should he, like a tragic poet, try to imagine the probable utterances of his characters or reckon up all the consequences probably incidental to the occurrences with which he deals, but simply record what really happened and what really was said, however commonplace.
>
> For the object of tragedy is not the same as that of history but quite the opposite. . . . In the one case it is the probable that takes precedence, even if it is untrue, the purpose being to create illusion to spectators; in the other it is the truth, the purpose being to confer benefit on learners.[35]

Polybius writes thus because he wants to denounce a growing tendency to assimilate history and tragic poetry still further. In particular, he wishes to attack Phylarchus (p. 111) for writing, apparently, history that was too close to tragedy, and appealing too much to the emotions, with the consequent sacrifice of accuracy. And Polybius considered the style of Timaeus to be that of 'third-rate historical tragedy',[36] although it must be confessed that when he himself wrote about King Philip II of Macedonia he was not guiltless of tragic history.

Cicero was well aware that history was not at all the same as poetry, as he makes clear in an imaginary discussion between himself and his brother Quintus.

> QUINTUS   As I understand it, then, my dear brother, you
> believe that different principles are to be followed in history and in poetry.

MARCUS   Certainly, Quintus. For in history the standard by
which everything is judged is the truth, while in poetry it
is generally the pleasure one gives.[37]

Cicero, who was human enough to describe his own consulship
as 'a drama'[38] (Caesar saw the whole of history in this light),[39] is
manifestly contradicting what was a tendency of his time. And it
was a tendency that continued. Sallust's *Catiline* is not so much
history, as the term would be understood today, as a dramatised
historical tableau, a tragedy.[40] Livy too, intent on his poetical
sweep, often divides his narrative into episodes reminiscent of the
textbooks on tragic drama, displaying dramatic contrasts in order
to promote emotional variety, and exhibiting a keen sense of theatrical detail; his sieges in particular display all the features of
drama.[41] Moreover, Quintilian openly concedes that history is very
close to poetry, indeed is a sort of poetry without restriction to
metre (*historia ... est proxima poetis, et quodam modo carmen
solutum est*).[42] Plutarch, too, saw life as an acted tragedy, and felt
that the historian needed 'dramatic characters'.[43] Yet he saw the
danger of tragic poetry to historians, for 'picking out people's
miseries'.[44]

As for Tacitus, he is described, we saw, as one of Rome's few
great poets; his purpose and technique are highly theatrical.[45] Look
at his language relating to Germanicus and Nero, and his account
of Nero's murder of his mother – patterned on the tragic story of
Clytemnestra and Orestes, or Agave and Pentheus. It is no surprise
to learn that when Tacitus was young he had written plays.[46]
Aelius Aristides compromised by seeing history as midway
between poetry and oratory, and Ammianus Marcellinus, when
something exciting occurred, remarked that 'the scene now
resembled a stage show'.[47]

All of these comparisons with epic and tragic poetry and with
the poetical theatre show how very different ancient ideas of historiography were from any that are held today.[48]

HISTORY AND RHETORIC AND PHILOSOPHY

Rhetoric

In its original Greek form, rhetoric was the systematic study of
public speaking, namely oratory.[1] It was the art of persuasion. The

poems of Homer had already shown how keen the Greek interest was in speech; but the first man to teach oratory was the Sicilian Corax, in the 460s BC. Another Sicilian, Gorgias of Leontini, introduced the new art – together with the concept that it could be taught – to Athens in 427 BC. Then rhetorical training, taught by the sophists, rapidly became the favourite form of more advanced education, and inevitably exercised a great influence on historiography. In the following century Plato and Isocrates dealt with the controversies that thus arose,[2] and Aristotle's *Rhetoric* went into many details. The development of rhetoric under the Hellenistic empires that followed was determined by the needs of the courts and schools.

In Roman times, the study of rhetoric gained new force. In the 'unreal atmosphere of the schools, with their mutual admiration and false values' – schools which virtually constituted such higher eduction as there was – and in this very oral/aural society, the power of rhetoric in great affairs became clearer. Rome, in the first century BC, was nauseated with political oratory; and then, in imperial times, rhetoric pervaded the whole of culture, and so pervaded the work of the historians. 'Roman historians drew on the devices taught in the schools of rhetoric to praise or discredit their subjects.'[3]

Thus, history was little more than rhetorical invention; capitulating to popular demand, historiography was essentially rhetorical – intended to entertain. That was why it was sometimes witty, barbed with anecdotal or epigrammatic humour. But it was also, at the same time, serious, because history and oratory had a single serious aim, the instruction of public opinion.[4] And it seemed that history could achieve this only by 'oratorical writing' – by producing an ordered, artistically composed whole, in keeping with the rules of rhetoric.[5]

Rhetoric changed a lot during the course of antiquity, but it always remained powerful – because ancient politics needed it.[6]

The fact that oratory flourished in the Greek *poleis* and at Rome was closely dependent, as the ancients well knew, . . . on the ways in which political matters were handled, on the organisation of the judicial system . . . . The art of persuasion was no more than the principal aspect of the process of informing the people of what they needed to know in order to come to a political or judicial decision – of moulding public opinion in general. . . . As a result, the history of oratory at Rome in the *Brutus* of Cicero turns out to be in large measure political history.[7]

Thucydides was a rhetorical historian, well versed in the theory and practice of the art, and responsible, on occasion, for 'rhetorical magnification'. He was therefore particularly appreciative of Pericles's ability to arouse and calm emotions by rhetorical means, seeing this as the duty of a public-spirited statesman. Xenophon, on the other hand, although originally an orator himself, was largely free of rhetoric, and Polybius was its relentless foe, attacking the speeches reported by Timaeus as being 'in the manner of someone trying to discuss a set theme in a rhetorical school'.[8]

Cicero tried to face up to the relationship between history and rhetoric, as he tried also to face up to the relationship between history and poetry. On the one hand, he saw and appreciated their close connection. Indeed, he believed that history was 'a kind of oratory' and owed a lot to rhetoric, and needed the embellishment that it could offer (though Atticus was reported as offering similar views 'with a smile'). On the other hand, Cicero felt that rhetoric might distort what emerged from the historians – and had not given them the help that it could. As he makes the orator Marcus Antonius say, 'Do you see how great a responsibility the orator has in historical writing? I rather think that for fluency (*flumine orationis*) and diversity of diction it comes first. Yet nowhere do I find this art supplied with any independent directions from the rhetoricians.'[9]

Livy 'had many of the deep-rooted defects of the rhetorical school',[10] from which (since he loved oratory and possessed pre-eminently the gifts of an orator) he adopted many devices, sacrificing (for example in his descriptions of battles) accuracy to style and rhetoric. Josephus tried to write in a relaxed manner embellished by rhetorical ornament, although he did so with some difficulty because Greek, in which he wrote, was not his mother tongue. Plutarch maintained that 'a rhetorical training would cover all forms of public utterance, narrative as well as argument' – although he took care to contrast rhetoric with history.[11]

Tacitus, who, as we saw, had been a good speaker when he was young,[12] was seriously involved in rhetoric.[13] His psychology fell into rhetorical stereotypes;[14] they made him an enforced, perhaps involuntary, liar. Indeed, one of the worst mistakes in his *Annals*, the erroneously dated account of Boudicca's rebellion in Britain, has rhetoric as its principal cause.[15] Earlier, his *Agricola* bears many of the marks of a rhetorical panegyric.[16]

The style of Suetonius was coloured by rhetoric, and the interest that he (like Plutarch) displays in physiognomy comes from the rhetorical schools.[17] Of the same origin, too, is Lucian's *How to Write History*, dismissed by M. I. Finley as a shallow and worthless rhetorical pot-boiler.[18] Aelius Aristides saw history as midway between poetry and oratory.[19] Much later, Ammianus Marcellinus was a combination of historian and rhetorician.[20]

All of this connection with rhetoric is undoubtedly a hindrance to our appreciation of ancient historiography as our main source for ancient history – though H. I. Marrou, in a sense, tried to defend its influence:

> Most modern readers, unless initiated into it, can neither grasp nor appreciate the subtlety of the ancient art [of rhetoric] . . . which reigned so tyrannically over classical education and so over classical literature.
>
> Was it beneficial or disastrous? Today the epithet 'rhetorical' is most often used with a pejorative connotation, the equivalent of bombastic, pompous, artificial. . . . We must react against this denigration of everything that may appear to be formal.[21]

Philosophy

Ancient philosophy and history cannot help being bracketed together, because they were the two main types of literature in artistic prose.[22] Yet, although Plato's *Republic* shows an interest in the philosophy of history,[23] and although Xenophon and Callisthenes had initially been philosophers,[24] most Greek practitioners of philosophy remained indifferent to history as a discipline.[25] History seemed to them to be rooted in that transient world of ambitions and passions from which philosophy was supposed to liberate humankind.[26]

Historians, on the other hand, were often prepared to pay homage to philosophy. Thus Polybius, although not an adherent of any school, knew something about philosophy, and criticised Timaeus for his ignorance of the subject.[27] The Stoics sought to exercise a certain control over historiography, and Posidonius strengthened their grip. But it would be a mistake to see Livy as subject to Peripatetic (Aristotelian) influence, as has been urged.[28] The same has been said, likewise dubiously, of Plutarch, who sometimes attempted philosophical discussion, and could be described as, at heart, a serious Platonist.[29]

As for ourselves, we should prefer nowadays to divorce historical studies from philosophy.[30]

HISTORY AND DOCUMENTS

We nowadays like our historiography to be supported by documents (pp. 118–22). This did not function in the ancient world, for two reasons. First, the documents and archives, whether public or private, were hopelessly inadequate and without meaning, even if relatively numerous (and in some cases of early date).[1] Second, the Greek and Roman historians did not care very much about these documents and rarely quoted or even paraphrased them.

> A work of literature, whether historical or not, had in the first instance artistic ends. One had therefore to adapt citations, whether of an earlier author, of a document or of an inscription. It is very rare for a citation, particularly a long one, to be verbatim.[2]

Take, for example, the case of Hellanicus (pp. 107–8):

> There were numerous stones at Athens, officially inscribed and precisely dated, from which, if they were all preserved, a modern student would probably construct without difficulty and with absolute certainty an exact chronicle of Athenian history in the fifth century. But it never occurred to Hellanicus to look for them, and in this he was only like most other Greek historians.
>
> If he had consulted a certain inscription, which we are fortunate enough to have recovered, he could have found that several military events which he chronicled occurred in the same archonship, corresponding to the latter half of 459 BC and the former half of 458 BC. Ignorant of this authentic evidence, he distributed these events over three archonships.[3]

The same applies to Thucydides. In spite of a number of citations that he offers, there are many more instances of his failure to quote relevant documents. Quota lists and tribute lists make up for some of his omissions. They show how very weak he was on Athenian finance.[4] By 1982, fifty-two inscriptions had been found at Athens recording Assembly decrees down to 321 BC.[5] But those relating to the period covered by Thucydides escaped his notice, or did not seem to him worth incorporating in his work.

Was the labour of deciphering them [inscriptions] too laborious?

It is remarkable that Thucydides describes a sixth-century inscription, which he quotes, as written 'in faint characters'. Yet a portion of that same inscription which has survived seems to a modern epigrapher quite clear, after more than two thousand years.[6]

In the case of Xenophon, too, finds of papyri (p. 121) correct his versions of events. Polybius attacks Timaeus (p. 110) for his mistaken employment of inscriptions, and boasts that he uses one himself. But he very significantly classes the investigation of documents in only third place as a provider of material to historians: 'the study of documents is only one of the three elements which contribute to history, and stands only third in importance.'[7] It is not surprising, therefore, that the 'decline' of Boeotia which he proclaims is, in fact, refuted by coins and inscriptions.[8]

Early Roman history is as bad as Greek in its absence of contemporary documents – especially public documents, since most records were in private archives. The gap was not filled by the Linen Books (*libri lintei*),[9] which, even if not forgeries as has been maintained, did not go back as far as the fourth century BC, as was thought.[10] True, two of the letters quoted by Sallust are said to be copies of actual documents.[11] But he, like most Roman historians, failed to search out documentary evidence. Of this failure Livy is a prime example. Although he is interested in early but still visible statues,[12] he does not consider it his job to conduct documentary research;[13] if he had, he might have used an inscription to correct what he said about the S. C. De *Bacchanalibus*.[14] And when Augustus in 29 BC manifestly misread or falsified an inscription in the temple of Jupiter Feretrius, in order to make a political point in relation to the antique Aulus Cornelius Cossus, Livy is aware that he is wrong, but refrains from openly contradicting him.[15] All of this shows a lighthearted attitude to the epigraphic evidence that would now be considered important.

Josephus quotes two letters of King Agrippa II – a unique gesture.[16] Tacitus, as we shall see (pp. 49–52), reports a speech of the emperor Claudius in terms which differ markedly from the actual text, which has been discovered; and that is not the only example of inscriptions correcting him.[17] He does, however, use official records directly. And Suetonius claimed to have studied letters personally, making use of verbatim documents, at least for earlier periods.[18] Plutarch, however, could be deceived by a falsification.[19] He was not alone in this; indeed, imperial documents are often spurious.[20]

It is the same with archaeology as it is with documents. We appreciate archaeology today, and realise that history largely depends on it, as a supplement and corrective to the ancient historians (cf. pp. 119–20). 'The advance of historical techniques', remarked K. J. Dover, 'has emancipated historians from dependence on historiography.'[21] But this was a discovery of the nineteenth century, when Michael Rostovtzeff's mastery of archaeological data caused surprise. Even now, in our own time, 'the potential of archaeology is vast and as yet unrealised'.[22] We hear of the 'new archaeology',[23] but it still has a long way to go. In ancient times, it had gone only a very short way indeed.

Archaeology has subsidiary branches which likewise proved of little interest to Greek and Roman historians (cf. pp. 118–22). Since their time, for example, papyri have been found in the Egyptian desert, and some of them correct what Xenophon told us.[24]

Coins, too, are a very valuable source of information about that world, although they naturally put forward the views of the governing authority which issued them. And that they do, during the Roman principate, in great variety and multiplicity,[25] contradicting or amplifying, on many occasions, what has been told to us by the literary authorities, who are largely unaware of them.

3

SOURCES AND STRANGENESS

SOURCES AND RUMOURS

Written Sources

Most of the famous historians had a wide, even if inadequate, range of written sources to draw upon.[1] Although this was not, as we shall see, so much the case with the early Greeks, who had to rely more upon people's memories, later on there was a great abundance of writings that could be consulted. Some of these are referred to in pp. 107–22.

The use of such materials by the notable historians varied. Sometimes they made a judicious choice of which source or sources should be followed. Sometimes the choice was less judicious. In certain cases they followed a single source, ignoring or rejecting the rest. In other cases they adapted the versions of more than one source, even if what they derived from those sources was contradictory. At times, they showed a liking for 'probability' as a criterion (pp. 42–4). Moreover, their practice as regards citing their sources varied. Sometimes we find a reference to an authority, but on other occasions such mentions are scrupulously avoided. None of this is in keeping with our modern preference for alluding to sources, perhaps in one of the footnotes which are a feature of modern, but not of ancient, historiography.

Herodotus, whose history looks oral because it was probably designed to be read in public,[2] lived at a time when the hard facts written down about the Persian Wars were few. Thucydides was sceptical about the literary evidence at his disposal, criticising 'the prose chroniclers, who are less interested in telling the truth than in catching the attention of their public, whose authorities cannot be checked, and whose subject-matter, owing to the passage of time, is mostly lost in the unreliable streams of mythology'.[3] When Xenophon admitted that he left out actions if they were 'not worth mentioning',[4] he may have meant that his written intelligence was unreliable. Polybius attacked Timaeus for being 'too bookish', that is to say for reading too much instead of having been personally involved in the action.[5]

Sallust hired secretaries to do most of his historical research.[6] Livy 'unquestionably reproduces errors and distortions from his sources which a better historian would have eliminated'.[7] Although he made perfunctory attempts to sift his material, he neither possessed, nor sought control over, earlier accounts. True, he was not unaware that his sources for antique history (most of which are now unavailable) tended to be worthless,[8] but he was too lacking in personal experience and too ignorant of practical politics to correct such stories. He was also guilty of mistranslations.[9]

It sometimes happens that he [Livy] relates the same event twice, presumably since it was reported in a different place in two texts. Some of Hannibal's Spanish operations appear to be repeated, and his crossing of the Apennines is reported twice – only as an attempt at the end of 218 and as a fact in the spring of 217. It is clearly an account of the same march, but Livy has not separated two sources which conflict over the date, but coalesced them.

A similar case is the defeat of Cnaeus Fulvius, which Livy ascribes first to be a praetor in 212 and then to a proconsul of the same name in 210 – without noticing that it is the same occurrence, for which his sources had given differing dates. The special election of the dictator Marcus Junius is also reported twice . . .

The granting of *provocatio*, the right of appeal from the decisions of a magistrate to the people as a whole, is recorded as having been made on three occasions, in 509, 449 and 300. There are reasons for thinking that the first two are unhistorical anticipations of the actual grant in 300. Similarly, there are two previous occasions (449 and 339) on which the provisions of the *Lex Hortensia* are said to have been introduced, and all cannot be correct . . .

He states that stage performances were first acted in the

Megalesia in 194, and then makes an identical claim for 191 . . .

The extent of Livy's mental confusion can be measured in Book xxviii, where the expulsion of the Carthaginians from Spain is dated first in the thirteenth year of the war, then in the fourteenth.[10]

[His] most culpable errors are those involving mistranslation, which can be detected by systematic comparison with the account of Polybius. . . . In [some] passages, Livy has misinterpreted whole sentences. . . . A clear and somewhat damning picture emerges of a mind rapidly and mechanically transposing the Greek, and coming to full consciousness only when grappling with the more congenial problems of literary presentation.[11]

Plutarch reverted to these bad practices of Livy, producing page after page which are just slavishly reproduced from earlier writers, and not bothering to trace his information back to its origins. Tacitus, who conducted extremely little independent research, quite often quotes the sources that were available to him – for example the memoirs of Agrippina the younger[12] – but does so unsystematically, since he repeatedly relocates and reorganises transmitted material.[13] In any case the stamp of his own personality is too strong for it to receive much attention.

Oral Tradition

Ancient society was much more oral/aural than our own.[14] This particularly applied to early times, when written authorities were so few and inadequate, but such poverty persisted: 'the insufficiency of primary literary sources is a continuing curse'.[15]

It imposed stringent limits on the would-be historian, as, indeed, it still does if one is trying to reconstruct the ancient world. However, there was continuing, touching faith in the oral tradition, although, for all its extensiveness, it was incomplete, contradictory, untrustworthy, and sometimes purely fictitious; which is why the younger Seneca made fun of it.[16] Many were the historians who were proud to have heard something 'from the horse's mouth', and they often showed insufficient appreciation that human memory plays disconcerting tricks. And, as for the remoter past periods that they were sometimes considering, such memories were virtually useless; it is not surprising that the ancients so often preferred contemporary history.[17]

Herodotus, uniquely successful in handling oral traditions, was always asking people to tell him things, and although he made mistakes he did not always believe what such people said.[18] Thucydides was particularly well aware of the need to obtain accurate spoken information and of the difficulty of acquiring it.[19] Although 'not privy to modern research on the hazards of oral history',[20] he stressed how important it was to be careful in the interrogation of eyewitnesses, who might well give quite different accounts from one another.[21] Xenophon drew on his own and others' memories, relating, often, to events that had occurred many years earlier. Polybius, as we saw, deplores bookishness in a historian, but is a little inconsistent in his attitude to eyewitnesses, although he fully maintains that enquiry and autopsy are necessary to his 'pragmatic' aim of recording such events as affected the political situation.[22] Livy (in his surviving books) and Tacitus were writing about things that had happened too long ago for any reliable oral tradition to have survived, though Tacitus was careful to contrast what had been handed down orally (*fama*) with the literary tradition (*auctores*).[23] As for Ammianus Marcellinus, he was writing in the later empire, when it was dangerous to write about contemporary events, so the less enquiry from eyewitnesses the better. In any case, most of the important decisions, for years past, had been taken in secret, so that first-hand information about them was impossible to acquire.

Rumours

In the largely oral societies of Greece and Rome it was inevitable that rumours should play an extensive part. The Greek historians were mostly alert to their possible or probable falsity. But rumours persisted all the same, and played their part in history and historiography. In Roman times they really came into their own. Sallust provides an unbroken series of unproven rumours, and the practice of Tacitus in this respect is persistent and lamentable. True, he rejected some rumours, and on occasion displayed scepticism towards them (especially if they were of popular and not aristocratic origin),[24] yet his willingness to accept many rumours impeded accurate history, and it was not helped by his reporting stories that he knew to be false.[25]

One feature very damaging to Tacitus's credit is the manner in which he employs *rumores*. Of course, a historian may properly report the state of public opinion at particular times, or use the views of contemporaries on major historical figures as a form of 'indirect characterisation' of them. But Tacitus often goes far beyond this...

He implants grave suspicions which he neither substantiates nor refutes. Their cumulative effect can be damning and distorting.... Time and again Tacitus is ready with an unpleasant motive, susceptible neither of proof nor of disproof.[26]

This last point brings us to innuendos, which are a particular feature of Tacitus's work, often presented as 'alternative explanations',[27] and particularly prominent in the unfair selectivity of his offensive picture of the emperor Tiberius. We do not concede that such innuendos are reputable history, but there were many ancients who thought differently.

In the *Annals* of Tacitus, they played a large part in the contradictions that emerge between facts and impressions,[28] which often appear virtually indistinguishable, although this, too, is harmful to the truth of the picture which is presented to us. Once again, the character and career of Tiberius provide conspicuous examples, but so, in the same reign, do the death of Germanicus and the subsequent trial of Cnaeus Calpurnius Piso.[29]

Predecessors

It is characteristic of human nature to criticise one's predecessors, and the Greek and Roman historians went in for this in a big way. They were encouraged by the literary principle that it was up to a writer to advance such criticisms in order to demonstrate that he himself was offering something new. But it results in some rather unattractive and undignified carping. However, 'every generation must rewrite history in its own way.'[30]

Thucydides stresses the inadequacies of earlier historians, and although he refrains from specifically criticising Herodotus – to whom he owed a great debt – he does so by implication. He notes two inaccuracies, sets right his predecessor's geography, stresses the scale of the Peloponnesian War in order to attack Herodotus's claims for the Persian War, and in general presents himself as Herodotus's successor, critic and rival.[31]

Although, as we shall see elsewhere, the motives of Polybius were mixed, he delivered a long, far-reaching and extremely varied criticism of Timaeus. He attacked Phylarchus as well (p. 111), regarding him as an emotionalist and a liar. However, he made use of what they both had said.[32]

Livy, too, found a predecessor, Valerius Antias, useful, although he meticulously listed his defects, including erroneous statistics.[33] And Josephus openly indicated his desire to supersede earlier writers.[34]

SELECTION

Obviously a historian has to select.[1] Not everything can be included. In the words of L. B. Namier, 'As no human mind can master more than a fraction of what would be required for a wide and balanced understanding of human affairs, limitation and selection are essential in the historian's craft.'[2] This is a particular necessity for historians of modern times, when the material is so vastly extensive.[3] However, it was already an urgent matter for their ancient predecessors, which they did not always handle very well. The surviving material sometimes has a random appearance.

A special trouble is that selection cannot possibly be wholly objective. It inevitably involves omission, shifted emphasis, personal choices of subject matter and sequence of facts, and distortion.[4] We cannot, therefore, obtain the whole, undoctored truth from any historian, and that particularly applies to historians in the ancient world, who had quite other matters at the top of their minds. Their historiography was necessarily conditioned by their own interest and vision.

> Any piece of historical writing, which has a minimum of political commitment and aims at least at some ideal, naturally attempts to establish its own interpretative approach in the reconstruction of the past, in the choice and elaboration of themes and facts, and in the organisation and disposition of the narrative. Some distortion of the past thus always takes place . . .
>
> Objectivity, even if achieved, was always confined within the narration of a chosen sequence of facts. This choice

42

corresponded to an established perspective, and was itself an act of interpretation.[5]

The difficulty becomes particularly acute after the times of Herodotus and Thucydides, when the authorities available had been relatively few. And epitomes of large works contribute to their subjectivity. Thus, not only does the pragmatism of Polybius make him eclectic,[6] but also it would be too much to expect reliability of balance among those who epitomised such a large part of his work.[7] Then in the first century BC people liked abridged history or 'famous passages', and Sallust's selection (and consequent distortion) took the form of deliberate dramatisation and impressive presentation, working up to a dramatic climax.[8] Josephus's life is full of misleading missions.[9]

As for Plutarch,

One cannot and must not expect from him what he did not intend to produce, a work of history.

The observation appears banal, but is not. It is clear enough that Plutarch not only used more or less fully the material he found useful, but also slanted and arranged it according to his general biographical interests.... This content was selected and arranged with quite different ends in view from those of the modern historian.[10]

Tacitus, too, omits, selects and abbreviates, on the explicit grounds, alluded to earlier, that 'some facts are not worthy of record'.[11] When he writes about the British revolt, as elsewhere, his omissions and selections are wholly intentional, aimed at brevity, speed and concentration.[12] His unfriendly presentation of Tiberius, too, is replete with unfair selectivity. When we come to Suetonius, the material at his disposal was particularly immense, and he had to select from it with all the skill he possessed, at least for the time of Augustus.[13]

Alternatives and Probability

When faced with two contradictory sources, the Greek and Roman historians all too often chose which they regarded as the more *probable* version. But this was sometimes wrong: verisimilitude is not always a good guide.

However, one of the most extraordinary things about Herodotus is his suspension of belief about some of these 'probable' stories that he tells. 'I am not obliged to believe it all alike,' he comments; 'a remark which must be understood to apply to my whole history.' For 'I'm reporting'; he says. 'I don't necessarily believe it.'[14] This is, in a way, salutary: he shows that he is not credulous. But it also means that, quite often, he offers alternative versions of a story, without necessarily making up his mind which is right. In other words, he suspends his own belief, and feels no firm obligation to tell the truth. The decision to believe or not believe rests not with himself but with his readers.[15] His own standard of what is credible and probable seems to waver, although he does tend to exclude what is physically impossible.[16] Nevertheless, he remains over-credulous of remote events and huge numbers.

Thucydides strongly favoured the 'probable', suppressing what he regarded as dubious allegations, and very rarely recording divergent accounts.[17] That is to say, he allows us no choice between versions; no access to his workshop is offered.[18] Polybius, as so often, has given the matter a good deal of thought. He sees the advantages of probability, although there are occasions, he recognises, when it may be untrue. On the whole, he concludes that probability is a good enough criterion for the tragedian, but not good enough for the historian, who needs the truth.[19]

Livy has been accused of being a little too prompt about accepting the early Roman legends, which, however, he sceptically realises may not be entirely accurate, although they have a sentimental and patriotic value: 'I have it in mind', he says, 'neither to affirm their truth nor to refute them' (*ea nec adfirmare nec refellere in animo est*).[20] But, despite his disclaimers, he is again tempted by 'probability'.[21] So is Plutarch, who thus conquers his unwillingness to decide which version to prefer.[22] Tacitus uses 'alternative explanations' to provide innuendos.[23] Suetonius, when confronted with two incompatible sources, fails to offer a consistent account.[24]

SPEECHES, DIGRESSIONS AND CYCLES

Speeches

The writings of the Greek and Roman historians are full of speeches.[1] They could not possibly have been delivered in the forms in which they were reported. For one thing, nobody had taken down full notes of them at the time, and there were no hand-outs describing their contents. Second, the language in which the historians reported them is very often their own, and not that of the speakers. Third, in the absence of loud-speakers, generals just did not, could not, address their whole armies.[2]

Nevertheless, partly because of the ancient significance of rhetoric (pp. 30–3),[3] speeches played a large part in every historical work. It was recognised that, for the reasons mentioned above, they were not accurate and exact representations of what had been said. But what the historians put down, as an alleged record of such speeches, was a vital part of ancient historiography, because it reflected the backgrounds and explanations of events and the characters, motives, intentions, aims, expectations and reactions of the principal participants. The speeches, therefore, with which the works of the ancient historians are filled form a vital part of their historical picture. Yet, in spite of fairly frequent protestations that they must be accurately reported, they are not history in the modern sense of the word, because they are unauthentic; if they ever took place at all, they were not delivered in those terms, or even with those contents. Thus, the speeches form an enormous barrier between ancient ideas of historiography and our own conceptions of the same activity.[4]

The origins of these speeches lie in the Homeric epic,[5] and Attic tragedy maintained the tradition. Herodotus, perhaps influenced by early tragedy (p. 26),[6] employed them to enliven his narrative and to convey judgements, but he did not imply that they were correct replicas of anything that had been said.[7] This, it must be repeated, they were not, as some ancients recognised.[8] The debate on constitutions (522 BC), ascribed by Herodotus to seven Persians, is obviously fictitious, designed to point the main themes of the book. And the famous meeting between Solon of Athens and Croesus of Lydia probably never took place.[9]

Thucydides was well aware that his reporting of speeches was not entirely factual; and this is what he said.

> In this history I have made use of set speeches, some of which were delivered just before and others during the war.
>
> I have found it difficult to remember the precise words used in the speeches which I listened to myself, and my various informants have experienced the same difficulty. So my method has been, while keeping as closely as possible to the general sense of the words that were actually used,

45

to make the speakers say what, in my opinion, was called for by each situation.[10]

P. A. Brunt interestingly speculates on what Thucydides was driving at when he created this sort of material.

> Why did Thucydides insert speeches? Probably it never occurred to him not to do so . . . .
>
> The speeches in Thucydides's work not only diversify the narrative but bring out vividly the conditions of actual life. Moreover, they make us feel that we are, as it were, in direct contact with the speakers . . . .
>
> The appearance of objectivity . . . is an illusion. . . . [Thucydides's speeches] are replete with abstract ideas, while often containing little that relates to the concrete situation. . . . In inventing [the speakers'] words, he makes them disclose their real thoughts and motives, or what he took to be such.[11]

C. M. MacLeod analysed his speeches in this way:

> [Thucydides's speeches] suggest, however obliquely, a judgement of the author's. They also invite the reader to frame one himself. He can do this in part from the speeches in themselves, by weighing their arguments and sifting the cogent from the plausible.
>
> But Thucydides's history is a complex of *logoi* [words] and *erga* [deeds], and if words are the teachers of deeds, no less may facts be the touchstone of words. A speech may be fatally mistaken like Alcibiades's, it may be tragically belied by events like the Funeral Speech, it may, like the Plataeans' speech, be a hopeless attempt to avert a predetermined doom. The speeches thus invite the reader's critical scrutiny, the result of which may be a sense not only of enlightenment, but of tragedy. For they move the reader by their fallibility no less than they illumine him by their penetration.[12]

J. Wilson goes into still further detail.

> I am asking here what kinds of moves his self-imposed rules allowed. . . . Among these kinds . . . are:
>
> 1 Reportage in his own style and not in the speaker's.
> 2 Selecting from a number of speeches actually made.

46

3 Selecting some of the γνώμη [i.e. basic significance of an individual speech] – not reproducing it all.
4 Not reproducing anything which does not count as γνώμη.
5 Adding words to make the γνώμη clearer.
6 Abbreviating or expanding (so long as the γνώμη is clear).
7 Casting the γνώμη (without changing its general force) in terms which might serve his particular purposes: for instance, the 'pairing' of remarks in two different speeches; or even their arrangement into a formal dialogue.[13]

Evidently Thucydides's speeches were important to him. There are forty of them, and they comprise 24 per cent of his whole work.[14] They are dramatic, and come at moments of decision, with the intention of making events intelligible. In these speeches, rising above mere literary convention, Thucydides makes use of his rhetorical knowledge in a sophisticated, sophistic and self-conscious way, creating a genre with laws and requirements of its own. The speeches teach lessons and manifest psychological insight, usually displayed in a crabbed version of his own language and not in that of the alleged speakers.[15] The writer produces the illusion of our being present ourselves. Yet the speeches are unauthentic, 'and the decision to include them is at odds with modern ideas of scientific historiography'.[16] They can be defended only on literary and artistic grounds. Thucydides is refashioning his subject matter in order to draw out its meaning. Indeed, it is of his own views, and of his own views of what happened, that the speeches are mouthpieces.[17]

They take several forms: four main categories have been noted.[18] Pericles's Funeral Speech is famous: written many years after its supposed delivery, it displays a retrospective, idealistic nostalgia for the old days, possibly presented with a certain veiled, sceptical irony, but designed, all the same, to refute anti-Periclean opinions. Whether it enshrines some utterances of Pericles himself is disputable.[19] Certainly it is a creation by Thucydides. The speech of the Syracusan Hermocrates is a prime example of an oratorical anachronism. The painful, moving Melian Dialogue is an invented dialectical treatise, even if the conference was ever held, as is uncertain.[20]

Xenophon's speeches are important, dramatic, and sometimes witty and well-argued,[21] but they, too, are fictitious. Plato failed to make a clear distinction between factual and invented discourse.[22]

Polybius expressed strong views about the need to reproduce speeches as accurately as possible (or, he might have added, to try to do so, because this could not always be done).

> The peculiar function of history is to discover, in the first place, the words actually spoken, whatever they were, and next to ascertain the reason why what was done or spoken led to failure or success. . . .
> But a writer who passes over in silence the speeches made and the causes of events and in their place introduces false rhetorical exercises and discursive speeches destroys the peculiar virtue of history.[23]

Polybius is therefore critical of Timaeus for his inaccurate reporting, or invention, of speeches.

> Can any of Timaeus's readers have failed to observe that his reports of these pronouncements disregard the truth and that this is done deliberately? The fact is that he has neither set down what was said, nor the real sense of what was said. . . .
> Now the special function of history, particularly in relation to speeches, is first of all to discover the words actually used, whatever they were, and next to establish the reason why a particular action or argument failed or succeeded.[24]

Elsewhere, Polybius accused Phylarchus, Chaereas and Sosylus of inserting fictitious speeches, 'gossip of the barber's shop', mere products of the rhetorical schools.[25] Yet his declaration that it was the peculiar function of history to discover the words that were actually spoken does not ring very impressively, because Polybius invents some speeches himself,[26] out of the total of thirty-seven found in the surviving parts of his work. No doubt he justified the procedure to himself on the grounds that they 'as it were sum up events' and 'hold the whole history together'[27] and he knew that, in Greek-speaking lands, speeches had a marked effect on actions.

Antonius, in Cicero's *On the Orator*, opened the way, by implication, to the invention of speeches when he pronounced that history demands 'not only a statement of what was done or said, but also the manner of doing or saying it'.[28] Even Caesar's orations are not authentic; though they are sometimes rendered in direct speech to give additional dramatic force.[29] Some of Sallust's speeches seem premature and unauthentic.[30] And when Sallust and

Livy employed direct discourse, Pompeius Trogus (p. 117) blamed it as illicit. Livy's speeches, although they are sometimes (but not always) well adapted to circumstances and speakers, and on occasion display psychological insight (mixed, however, with chauvinism), are nevertheless not 'substantially trustworthy', even in the later periods, but purely fictitious.[31] Josephus, too, fabricated speeches with particular lavishness, employing improbable pseudo-Jewish language.[32] Plutarch, also, reported speeches which, even if 'true to life', were by no means faithful reproductions of anything that was actually said.

By an extraordinary coincidence we possess not only Tacitus's account of a speech made by the emperor Claudius in the Roman senate but also the text of the actual speech itself, preserved on a bronze tablet at Lyon (Lugdunum). 'It is not very often that we are able to look over the shoulder of an ancient writer and see how he wields paste and scissors and box of paints.'[33] Here is part of the text of the speech:

> First let me rebut the first and obvious objection to a policy of generosity – that it is a new and unprecedented step. In fact, Roman constitutional history is full of innovation from the very beginning.
>
> Originally Rome was governed by kings, but not by a hereditary dynasty, for among them were men of new families and foreign extraction. Numa, for example, the second king, was a Sabine; Priscus Tarquinius came from Tarquinii in Etruria, where he was barred from office because of his birth (his father was a Corinthian immigrant, and his mother a noble but poverty-stricken Tuscan). Between Priscus and Superbus intervened Servius Tullius, son of a captive woman or a refugee from Etruria (if we may so interpret the evidence), yet proving an excellent king.
>
> After the expulsion of the kings came the annual magistrates of the Republic, the consulship, for instance, itself superseded in time of crisis by the dictatorship. *Tribuni plebis* were created to champion the plebs; consuls were replaced by decemvirs, and decemvirs by consuls. Yet again, the power of the consuls was distributed among the *tribuni militum*. The plebeians gained equality with the patricians.
>
> Our empire was extended by war – but as this would lead

up to the conquest of Britain I say nothing of this topic – and our citizenship offered to non-citizens. . . .

Augustus and Tiberius appointed senators from a wide field, but Italy retained and, as I shall show by my censorial *lectio senatus*, continues to retain the most prominent position. This, however, is not a reason for rejecting meritorious provincials.

Individual senators already come to us from colonies in the provinces, e.g. from Vienna in Gallia Narbonensis. Vestinus from that city is my trusted servant, and his sons should be able to look forward to a senatorial career. I say nothing of that fantastic man who irregularly secured the consulship; but Vestinus's brother is fully worthy of admission to your number.

In my review I have now reached, in logic and geography, the extremity of Gallia Narbonensis, and it is time to come to the point at issue.

Here is a deputation of nobles from Gallia Comata. You will have no regrets if they are made senators, any more than Paullus Fabius Persicus is ashamed of the title Allobrogicus won by his ancestor Quintus Fabius over doughty Gallic foes. You are glad to have members from Lugdunum, and here are your new recruits, from the countryside of the provinces beyond the Narbonese.

I have summoned up my courage to champion the cause of Gallia Comata as a whole, for the frontier which separates the old province from the rest is quite unreal; we, as a senate, must take the vigorous action in this matter.

It may be that the Gauls fought the deified Julius for ten years. But contrast with those ten years the hundred years of loyal service. For example, they preserved peace and quiet during the critical census of my father Drusus, although this was then a novel imposition and Drusus was called away to repel invasion. How responsible a task the holding of a census is I am realizing myself, though my task is lighter than his – I have merely to see that our resources become publicly known and receive public recognition.[34]

Here is Tacitus's version of the same oration, which is remarkably different.

The experience of my own ancestors, notably of my family's

Sabine founder Clausus who was simultaneously made a Roman citizen and a patrician, encourage me to adopt the same national policy, by bringing excellence to Rome from whatever source. For I do not forget that the Julii came from Alba Longa, the Coruncanii from Camerinum, the Porcii from Tusculum; and, leaving antiquity aside, that men from Etruria, Lucania and all Italy have been admitted into the senate; and that finally Italy herself has been extended to the Alps, uniting not merely individuals but whole territories and peoples under the name of Rome.

Moreover, after the enfranchisement of Italy across the Po, our next step was to make citizens of the finest provincials too. We added them to our ex-soldiers in settlements throughout the world, and by their means reinvigorated the exhausted empire. This helped to stabilise peace within the frontiers and successful relations with foreign powers. Is it regretted that the Cornelii Balbi immigrated from Spain, and other equally distinguished men from southern Gaul? Their descendants are with us; and they love Rome as much as we do.

What proved fatal to Sparta and Athens, for all their military strength, was the segregation of conquered subjects as aliens. Our founder Romulus, on the other hand, had the wisdom – more than once – to transform whole enemy peoples into Roman citizens within the course of a single day. Even some of our kings were foreign. Similarly, the admission to former office of the sons of slaves is not the novelty it is alleged to be. In early times it happened frequently.

'The Senonian Gauls fought against us', it is objected. But did not Italians, Volsci and Aequi, as well? 'The Gauls captured Rome', you say. But we also lost battles to our neighbours – we gave hostages to the Etruscans, we went beneath the Samnites' yoke. Actually, a review of all those wars shows that the Gallic war took the shortest time of all. Since then, peace and loyalty have reigned unbroken. Now that they have assimilated our customs and culture and married into our families, let them bring in their gold and wealth rather than keep it to themselves.

Senators, however ancient any institution seems, once upon a time it was new! First, plebeians joined patricians in

51

office. Next, the Latins were added. Then came men from other Italian peoples. The innovation now proposed will one day be old: what we seek to justify by precedents today will itself become a precedent.[35]

It is perfectly clear that Tacitus has rewritten and reorganised the entire speech, as K. Wellesley remarked.

The brutal fact is that only with the greatest difficulty can we find any resemblance at all to the original. The historian [relapses] into the more congenial atmosphere of imagination released from the shackles of fact. . . . It is difficult to imagine a more arbitrary or wilful literary device. . . .

We can find but three themes common to the original and to the copy – the theme of the acceptance of innovation (placed first by Claudius, but last by Tacitus), that of the value of foreign immigrants, and that of the shortness of the Gallic War. . . . But how much else has he bungled or neglected! How soon the juxtaposition of the two speeches reveals the weaknesses of the copy!

These are, in the main, four: first, the entire suppression of any characteristic features of Claudius's style; second, the omission of arguments that should be there; third, the addition of others which should not be there; and, fourth, an order of topics which is neither faithful to the source nor intelligible to the reader.[36]

Whether Tacitus had seen, or heard, what Claudius actually said is scarcely relevant. Nor is the question whether he had improved upon the emperor's words, or made them, on the contrary, less effective. The fact remains that the similarity of his supposed 'reproduction' to the original speech is minimal.

The same presumably applies to all of the speeches reported by Tacitus: whatever praise may be accorded them as literary or psychological achievements, they have been unkindly, but not altogether unfairly, compared to the fancies of a historical novelette. Wellesley concludes:

Tacitus has very little interest in reconstructing what really happened. His aim, throughout, is to point a moral (not always a very profound one) and adorn a tale. The purpose of the speeches is to clarify obscure and debated issues, or to add reflections and soliloquies when a decision is about to be taken. A speech gave an opportunity to expound a theme, or to show a personality in depth. . . . Speeches also add variety.'[37]

Of course the orations reported by the early Christians likewise bear little or no relation to anything that was actually said. In the four Gospels, for example, it can scarcely be supposed that the sayings attributed to Jesus were really and exactly his own words. In any case, one Gospel differs from another.

Digressions

A further main reason why ancient historiography differed from its modern counterparts was provided by digressions. They were far more frequent in Greek and Roman writings than in our own. For one thing, there was a simple technical explanation for such digressions. Nowadays we have footnotes; the ancients did not, so that what would now be relegated to a footnote had to appear in the text. But there was also a deeper philosophical explanation. The Greek and Roman historians wanted to supply background. For this reason, when, for example, an army invaded Thrace, it was considered appropriate and necessary to supply a digression, describing the country and its people. The idea goes back to the Homeric epic (pp. 25–7), and the digressions of Herodotus, for example, are an epic feature, deliberately designed. Polybius offers particularly numerous polemical digressions. Cicero specifically names digressions as one of the fairest fields for rhetoricians in their historical writing.[38] Livy rejects ornamental digressions, but indulges in them all the same.[39]

   In Plutarch, digressions abound, because he, a man with time at his disposal, was writing for leisurely people. 'He digressed out of the sheer exuberance of his interest and the richness of his knowledge.'[40] But he is aware that the practice must not be allowed to get out of hand, because 'such digressions are less likely to meet with condemnation from impatient critics if they are kept within bounds.' Nevertheless, his deviations include an extraordinarily wide range of themes: Greek and Roman religious festivals and rites, philological enquiries and attempted etymologies of Greek and Latin words, meteors and shooting stars, the causes of a disease called *boulimia* involving ravenous hunger, the names of Greek and Roman months, Roman divorce, underground water-channels, the Atlantic islands, the volume and power of the human voice, the temple of Jupiter Capitolinus, ghosts and miracles and portents, Archimedes and the history of mechanics, the introduction of wine among the Greeks.

It has been commented that the digressions in Ammianus Marcellinus seem out of place. But it appears, from what we have seen, that ancient readers did not feel the same.

Inevitability

The belief in inevitability is a great hindrance to accurate historiography, because in fact there is no such thing; what happens is due to human beings, and to their avoidable achievements and errors.[41] The Marxists have done the most to help this nonsensical doctrine to prevail. In ancient times, however, it did seem to many that there was something inevitable, or at least irresistible, about the rise and power of the Roman empire; Polybius was not altogether immune from this view, and I doubt if Livy and Tacitus would have dissented from it. About the non-inevitability of the Fall of the Roman empire I have written elsewhere.[42]

Cycles

Another, related, damaging element in historical thought is the cyclical theory – the view that there will always be historical recurrences.[43] Once again, this is not the real point, which is that recurrences, or anything else that may happen, are not inevitable at all but depend on what human beings have been able or unable to do.

Nevertheless, Herodotus and Thucydides were not averse to the cyclical idea,[44] nor was Plato. Polybius was sure that whatever grows must decline, according to the inevitable biological pattern, and whatever flourishes must fade.[45] That is, of course, by no means invalid, as far as it goes; nothing lasts for ever. Yet how long things last, it must be repeated, depends on the human agencies which direct the course of events. Thus, Tacitus was not accurate when he wrote: 'Perhaps not only the seasons but everything else, social history included, moves in cycles.'[46] This suggestion introduced, or encouraged, popular theory, which has subsequently been perpetuated by Vico and others.[47]

RELIGION AND PORTENTS

Another difficulty in the path of our understanding and acceptance of ancient historiography, another obstacle hindering our appreciation of what really happened, is provided by religion. True, religion has played a great part in shaping historical events,[1] but some find it difficult today to believe that it was God, or the heavenly powers, who guided this development of events.[2] People find it particularly hard in this twentieth century to accept the existence of an all-powerful God when happenings such as the holocaust have taken place. Yet, apart from this, the whole tendency of modern historiography, even among the religiously inclined, has been to search out human causes for human developments; to conclude that, when things have gone right or wrong, that is because human beings have made them so.

In these circumstances, modern men and women are unimpressed and confounded when Greek and Roman historians, unwilling or unable to find out the true human causes, have credited the course of events to the heavenly powers. Thus Herodotus, even if some of his remarks do not seem to support divine causation, saw the hand of God continually at work – jealously and fatefully punishing ambition, impiety and conceit, and pulling down the mighty and preserving a balance.[3] On the whole, even if he had little to do with the plain man's gods – influenced as he was by the Ionian enlightenment – he does believe in, and often stresses, divine intervention and causation.[4] This he sees as exemplified by the Persian War. He refrains from drawing too hard a line between the human and divine, but perhaps reveals a little sceptical irony,[5] which, according to one suggestion, he could not display more openly because he was afraid of charges of blasphemy.[6] This cannot be confirmed, and it seems clear that Herodotus, even if he found the divine power incomprehensible, believed in its intervention, and believed in oracles as well, although he sometimes distrusted them.[7] He believed that heaven declared what was to come not only in signs and portents and oracles and omens[8] but also in dreams, which, like many ancients from Homer onwards, were held by him to foreshadow future events.[9] He was also convinced that there is an inescapable Fate.[10]

We must not, however, overestimate this emphasis by ancient historians on religious factors.

The direction given by Herodotus and even more by Thucydides to history-writing certainly presupposes – and helps to reinforce – the assumption that the intervention of gods in human affairs is neither constant nor too patient.... Even in later centuries the marginal importance of gods in historical narrative presupposes, rather than expresses, Greek lack of interest in theological speculations.... Metaphysical explanations were, as a rule, either avoided or only briefly hinted at.[11]

Thucydides excluded divine intervention, though conditioned by many traditional beliefs, but was willing enough to blame Fortune (Tyche) when human error was the real cause. Polybius is largely rational, though with reservations. He feels that Timaeus allowed himself to include far too many prodigies and wonders.[12] But what is notable about Polybius is that he understood the social value of religion, by which standard Gaius Flaminius (consul 223 BC), for example, failed.[13] And Polybius allotted a dominant role to Fortune.[14] This represented a way of avoiding any wholehearted religious or philosophical commitment, and is salutary in that it recognised how history is often decided by accidents. Such a solution, however, can be damaging in that it provides too ready an answer when human explanations seem too hard to find – although they were, in fact, there, if it had been possible to find them, for example in respect of the rise of Rome. Cicero also has a good deal to say about the changes and chances of Fortune.[15]

Livy goes right back to piety. He sees '*no* hard line between the human and the supernatural' – which thus returned to history with a vengeance – and concedes the fateful intervention of divine forces. He is deeply involved in ritual,[16] and if taxed would have said that there was at least a 'symbolic truth' in his convictions.[17] These included a quasi-religious belief in Rome itself and its Fate: he was a living examplar of devotion to Romanness. He also offered a full and colourful catalogue of prodigies. Possibly he saw them as 'symptomatic of a disordered universe'.[18] But one wonders, once again, if he was truly reverent, or saw the current belief in them as a historical phenomenon, which it was; if he was keeping his finger, as it were, on the public pulse.[19] One wonders all the more when one reads what he says about the assertion that the father of Romulus and Remus had been the god Mars, who visited Rhea Silvia: 'Either because she believed it, or because a god was a more honourable agent of her disgrace, she named Mars as the father of her dubious offspring.'[20]

In other words, Livy here goes beyond his original intention of neither accepting nor rejecting such stories, and is actually ready to reject the present tale, although he does not quite do so. On another level, however, he wants to keep the legend, because it says something that he wants to say, and in this sense is worth holding on to. It is true, that is, that the Romans are truly the sons of Mars: one only has to look at their record in war to accept this.

Josephus, so strong an advocate of the Jews, was weak on comparative religion.[21] It has been suggested that Plutarch's disapproval of Herodotus was largely due to the latter's relative religious cynicism, which he did not share.

Tacitus was sweepingly sceptical about the supernatural, which was uncommon.[22] Tertullian attacked his slanders against the Jews, and his hostility towards the Christians.[23]

Christian historians, meanwhile, made up for this in full by making the whole of past history religious. Ammianus Marcellinus, on the other hand, held profound pagan convictions. However, this was a sensitive issue for him, under the Christian emperor Theodosius I, and Ammianus avoids religion in Books 26–31 of his History.[24]

TOO LITTLE ECONOMIC AND SOCIAL HISTORY

Economic History

In general, the Greek and Roman historians did not share, or foreshadow, the modern view, dating back to Marx and Weber in the nineteenth century, that economic history is exceedingly important.[1] They were aware, many of them, of economic factors, but they regarded them as altogether less significant than political developments; and there were few ancient statistics.[2]

> There is no doubt that history in antiquity, in the context of the problems which it analysed, favoured military, political and institutional affairs.
> It is open to question, however, whether economic affairs are really missing altogether. One may answer both yes and no. In our sense of the term, they are missing; one never

finds economic affairs at the centre of historical analysis or as the central element in historical narrative.[3]

The question arises in an arresting way when we consider Thucydides, who is by no means blind to economic influences.

Writing, for example, about early Greece, he stresses its lack of material resources. He also emphasises that the power of the Athenians depended on financial strength.

And he gives a detailed survey of their assets at the beginning of the Peloponnesian War. However, he decided that the war's main underlying cause was not economic at all, but political. . . . The real, basic cause was Sparta's political fear.[4]

In other words, believing as he did that economic factors were only secondary, he was sometimes weak in dealing with them, for example in regard to Athenian finance (on which inscriptions sometimes correct him).[5] To repeat the generalisation in the last paragraph, he was not unaware of this economic element but chose to reject it as an explanation, just as he omitted a good many other things as well.

Polybius, it can be justly said, although he was deeply interested in causation, was not attentive enough to economic causes. Livy's work contains a unique amount of economic information, although, like other ancient historians, he is not really alive to the significance of the economic factor,[6] maintaining a loud silence, for example, about the economic vicissitudes of early Rome.[7]

True, Roman historiography, on the whole, is more aware of economic developments than Greek.[8] But emperors did not really understand them, and they are conspicuously absent from Tacitus, who is, for example, very bad on German salt production.[9] The trouble was that ancient historians knew too little about the economy of the Roman empire; not that they cared about this lack of knowledge.

As a result, we are poorly informed, in detail, about the economy of the Roman world. There are no government accounts, no official records of production, trade, occupational distribution, taxation. A systematic account of the Roman economy is therefore beyond our reach. Economic historians, more even than those historians with traditional interests, must set themselves limited objectives, and exercise imagination and discrimination in their pursuit of them.[10]

It is very difficult for us, therefore (and the ancient historians did not even try), to keep pace with the fact that the basis of the Roman economy, and thus of the empire itself, was agriculture.

Despite the growth of urban and semi-urban settlements throughout the Empire, it is probably true to say that by far and away the greater proportion of the population dwelt in the country and engaged in rural activities. The empire's economy was firmly linked with agriculture . . . .

Primarily, the empire depended on adequate grain production, but wine, olive oil, wool, leather and meat were all important to the economy. . . . The primacy of land both as a measure of status and a form of investment was never doubted in the ancient world.[11]

If we look at other ancient cultures, it becomes clear that the Bible, for example, is quite uninterested in economic causes.

Social History

Turning to social history, we find that this too has become extremely fashionable, and is indeed regarded as essential today,[12] since it should and does provide information about social structures and changes, about art, and about women and workers and slaves, and about society from below. All of this too was, to our minds, neglected in the ancient world, in which there was greater interest in wars.

Aristotle, it must be said, collected an enormous amount of social history. Polybius, on the other hand, was not very attentive to such matters. Although he understood the social values of religion, in which, as we have seen (p. 56), he was in his own way interested, he eliminated cultural happenings.

Livy's social information is as abundant as his economic material, though he did not realise its importance. Tacitus is a good example of the omission of social history on the grounds that, although history should illuminate the contemporary world, social history was not part of the great narrative that he was setting himself to write. He omitted social details, too, because he supposed that his readers were already aware of them. Besides, he felt contempt for slaves and freedmen and the lower classes generally;[13] dignified classical historians do not speak of servants and fishermen in the way that the New Testament does.

The social views of Ammianus Marcellinus were mixed. He hated the members of the Roman upper class, who he felt were uncultured and were not doing their job – and who had not sufficiently welcomed him in the imperial city. But he also, like Tacitus, viewed the lower classes with the utmost dislike.

Ammianus wishes he was not obliged to refer to the lower classes at all. He feels constrained to apologise for the excessive length at which he has to describe 'nothing except riots and taverns and other similar vulgarities', themes he evidently regards as below and beneath the elevated level appropriate to history.

The fact is that he feels the strongest distaste for the enormous unprivileged sections of society.... Their coarse behaviour disgusts him. [It] 'prevents anything memorable or serious from being done in Rome'.[14]

4

MISINFORMATION AND MISTAKES

LOVE OF A STORY

Of course the historians of Greece and Rome, if they had any success, told an exciting story. If they were going to beguile their audiences with a public reading, as was often the case, the story had to be good and gripping. The distinction between *aphegesis* (story) and *historia* (history), even if valid, was not invariably made.[1] After all, what was the use of a history if it was not attractive enough to receive any attention? And if it was to receive attention it had to tell an interesting tale. As in other respects (pp. 25–7), Homer was not a bad model. The Homeric art of story-telling included conversations (pp. 44–53),[2] but the trouble was that indulgence in this art, by the historians, developed a 'tendency to deviate from strict truth in the interest of a good story'.[3]

The greatest story-teller of all time was Herodotus, and many of the stories for which he had such a wonderful flair were flippant and patently untrue.[4] It was probably to this talent or tendency that he owed the title of *mythologos*, a teller or weaver of tales.[5]

The gracious garrulity with which he tells historical anecdotes is one of the charms which will secure him readers until the world's end.

Gibbon happily observed that Herodotus 'sometimes writes for children and sometimes for philosophers'; the anecdotes he relates often appeal to both. . . . The contrast of the naïvety of Herodotus with his scepticism imparts to his epic a very piquant quality.[6]

61

M. I. Finley, however, was keen to play down this story-telling naïvety of Herodotus.

> Herodotus had a most subtle mind, and the story he told was complex, full of shadings and paradoxes and qualifications.... Nothing could be more wrong-headed than the persistent and seemingly indestructible legend of Herodotus the charmingly naïve storyteller.[7]

As for Xenophon, he was more of a story-teller than a historian, and exercised a strong influence on the Greek novel.[8] Polybius was well aware that he himself was writing at a time when history meant little more than wonder-stories. He was opposed to this.[9]

Tacitus denounced 'romance' in history.[10] However, he told some remarkable and not entirely truthful stories himself, notably, in the *Annals*, the tale of Agrippina the younger's death, and the account of the nasty Poppaea – a few stories about dreadful women did not come amiss. In addition, there was the invented narrative of the petition of Sejanus to Tiberius, and the equally fictitious appeal of Narcissus to Britannicus.

SELF-JUSTIFICATION

It is, unfortunately, almost inevitable that people should want to justify what they themselves have done in the past. Today we see it on every side. Writers are in a particularly good position to put forward such retrospective claims and accounts, and historians are far from immune from the desire to do so.[1] This is especially apparent among ancient historians, who by no means efface themselves.[2] Nor did the politicians who lived among them. The Athenian Solon, for example, largely focused his narrative of recent events upon his own political actions.[3]

Thucydides was probably drawing on his personal experiences as a commander when he imagined the thoughts of another general, Nicias. And it does appear that Thucydides, who makes such play with his wish to remain objective, disliked the statesman and financier Cleon not only on objective grounds but also for personal reasons: Cleon seemed inferior to his predecessors (being a member of the merchant class which wanted radical democracy) but Cleon also had led the way in pronouncing Thucydides's condemnation to exile after the latter had failed to save Amphipolis from the Spartan Brasidas.[4] That is what Marcellinus's *Life of*

Thucydides declares,[5] and although certainty eludes us it does seem probable that this is a correct explanation.[6] Certainly Thucydides loathes Cleon,[7] with an aversion that was unusual for him and unfair, and one of the causes is surely that he held Cleon largely responsible for his banishment. Cleon may well have urged his condemnation to this fate in the Assembly, but in any case Thucydides

> owed his exile to Cleon's abandonment of the Periclean restraint – since Brasidas would hardly have been allowed to reach Thrace in the summer of 424 and, if he had, Thucydides and his colleague Eucles would have been reinforced, had the Athens of Cleon been less distracted by the abortive Boeotian campaign.[8]

For the same reason, notably his banishment, it was already seen in ancient times that Thucydides was full of ill-will towards Athens.[9] This comes out in his (and its) treatment of the unhelpful island of Melos, which is not very fairly handled by Thucydides. Thus, he was not as objective as has been maintained, and was capable, for personal reasons, of offering savage views.

Xenophon's *Anabasis* is obviously full of self-defence and self-praise, to justify what he had done and to rescue himself from neglect.[10] By the same token, his picture of another Greek leader, Menon, is wholly defamatory, because of private enmity.[11] Xenophon's writings, and their publication, gave him the opportunity to ram home his personal, controversial standpoints, in the face of his critics and enemies. Not unnaturally, therefore, these endeavours became the models for later autobiographies – and for their efforts to disguise the fact that they were really propaganda. In the fourth century BC this custom of writing 'apologetic' pamphlets became established. Later, Aratus of Sicyon (271–203 BC) composed a famous, unreliable political memoir intended to explain and justify his own actions.[12]

The dislike of Polybius for Timaeus, to which reference has been made, was also partly personal. It

> sprang from a number of reasons.... He disliked and resented an author who was widely regarded as the first Greek historian of Rome, and so constituted a serious challenge to his own position.... [He had] a decided propensity

for malice, often directed against his predecessors for motives other than those he alleges.[13]

Personal motives came to loom large in Latin writings, too, some of which are now lost. Gaius Gracchus wrote a not entirely truthful *Life* of his brother Tiberius,[14] and Sulla composed an autobiography containing blatant self-praising inventions. Cicero was well aware of the possible untruthfulness of eulogistic writings.[15] That did not prevent him, however, from urging Lucceius to write an exaggerated account of his consulship:

> So I frankly ask you again and again to eulogise my actions with even more warmth than perhaps you feel, and in that respect to disregard the canons of history; and... of your bounty to bestow on our love even a little more than may be allowed by truth.[16]

As for Julius Caesar's 'Commentaries', both his *Gallic War* and his *Civil War* provide valuable information but they are extremely potent, subjective and clever works of self-advertisement and personal propaganda, disguised beneath apparent self-restraint and modesty. Their real aim is to avenge personal insults, and in the process we find Caesar quietly taking the credit for successes that his subordinates had won, blaming setbacks (such as Gergovia) on others and not on himself, and explaining that his apparent aggressions (notably the invasion of Britain) were not really unjustified aggressions at all.[17]

Sallust's brilliant historical works are almost wholly motivated by his own frustrations and failures, including attacks on his personal enemies, such as Marcus Aemilius Scaurus,[18] and leave behind a strong taste of sour grapes. Pollio's attack on Livy's *Patavinitas* (pp. 116–17) was partly personal, because Pollio had a grudge against the historian's home town of Patavium.[19] Josephus was a passionate hater of persons. He provides much self-praise and self-defence and openly admits that he is writing out of personal motives, in order to combat the criticisms of Justus. His attempts to do so, however, are not altogether convincing.[20]

As for Tacitus, he was never able to forget, or let us forget, that under the hated tyrant Domitian (81–96) he had connived at unforgivable murders, or had at least remained silent when they were committed, thereby advancing his own career. This is a consciousness which influences and handicaps his historical works.[21]

The passionate intensity of his writing stems from deeper psychological sources. Perhaps his own shame and even guilt are reflected in his passionate, but ambivalent, reactions to those who stand up to the tyrants.

Some scholars have gone much further and claimed to find evidence of the historian's melancholia, sadism, femininity, homosexuality, paranoia, or even madness. Though such claims are exaggerated, it is easy to see how critics can be led astray. . . .

His own political accommodation suggests greater ambiguity than a superficial reading of his histories will provide.[22]

Ammianus Marcellinus introduced a personal factor by being too favourable to his old chief Ursicinus.[23] His hostility to other members of the upper class (p. 60) is partly motivated by his belief that he had been cold-shouldered by Roman society.

INFLUENCES

Family Pressure

The influence of families and genealogies weighed heavily on ancient historians. All aristocracies love genealogies, and every prominent family had its own hereditary axe to grind, and made the historians aware of it. This was not difficult to do, since all ancient history (perhaps all history) is the history of the ruling oligarchy, and the ancients stressed that character depended partly on lineage.[1]

When Hecataeus spoke slightingly about the mythical stories of the Greeks, it has been suggested that genealogical traditions were what he particularly had in mind.[2] These were powerful at Athens, where friction between the leading families raged. And it would be unreasonable to suppose that Herodotus, coming in from outside, was immune to them. Indeed he does, on some occasions, display sympathy with the Alcmaeonid house, although Thucydides is more reserved and judicious concerning such matters.[3]

Polybius, coming to Rome, could not fail to support the cause of the Scipio family that had taken him up. At Rome family traditions were a serious matter, reflected in ancestral portrait busts, *laudationes funebres* and *elogia* that remained in family archives, and fraudulent noble genealogies.[4] This rubbed off obviously on to the historians, who were mainly members of the ruling class themselves,[5] so that the annalists show strong family biases. Cicero notes the historical distortions which this situation caused.[6] They are particularly apparent in Livy, who defers to earlier personages who were supposedly his own ancestors, while displaying hostility to the *gens Claudia*.[7] In general, he gives prominence to families, without displaying much insight into their untruthful manoeuvres, so that the family interests of his sources lead him into a good deal of misinformation.[8] (Augustus, according to Suetonius, encouraged this sort of ancestral veneration by honouring earlier great men).

Livy, because or although he was of provincial origin, was deeply impressed by Roman family pedigrees. Similar origins seem to have had just the opposite effect on Tacitus.[9] Nevertheless, he was prejudiced and enslaved by class and rank, and was not immune to the sedulous cultivation of dead forerunners which prevailed in his day.[10]

Politics

One of the main reasons why the ancient historians were biased was provided by politics. Above all, most of their writings were concerned with political issues. It was they who created the concept that history is largely a political matter. This was an idea which held the fort for ages, and was repeated and amplified and given canonical status in the nineteenth century. 'History', said John Seeley, 'fades into mere literature when it loses sight of its relation to practical politics ... history is past politics, and present politics future history.'[11] We do not agree with the comprehensiveness of that remark today, but it was how the Greek and Roman historians felt. They created the doctrine, now contested, that history is mainly concerned with politics (and military actions, pp. 76–80): man, as Aristotle observed, is a political animal. Besides, the ancient historians were very often vigorously partisan.

Thus, Herodotus could not fail to become involved in the politics of Athens when he went there, and his ambivalent attitude to the Alcmaeonids suggests this.[12] He was also lukewarm about Themistocles, for the same reason.[13] Thucydides, although not unaware of economic factors, believed that the underlying guidance of events was political.[14] It was under him that history became primarily political history; and this 'political fetish' meant that non-political and non-military factors tended to be omitted and ignored.[15] (He also gives a very incomplete picture of the domestic political scene inside Athens itself, when it does not seem to him particularly relevant to the major political event of the age, which was the Peloponnesian War).[16]

Xenophon writes as a political oligarch, and he also hates Thebes: he pointedly ignores its hero Epaminondas.[17] When Polybius calls history 'pragmatic', he means that it is primarily concerned with events directly affecting the political situation: he stresses that his work is a case-book for politicians. And he shows himself heavily involved in Greek politics, favouring the Achaean League and Macedonia, and disliking the Aetolian League, as well as Sparta. That is why he attacks Phylarchus (p. 111), because the latter supported the Spartan king Cleomenes III against the Achaean Aratus.[18] Polybius also assails Theopompus, for criticising Philip II of Macedonia.[19] However, he fails to sense the nuances of Roman public life.[20]

Politics were very much to the fore in the writings of Rome, where Gaius Gracchus wrote a partisan biography of his brother Tiberius (see above). Such polemical pamphlets were now abundant.[21] Cicero, although eager (in principle) to uphold the necessity of historical truth, urged Lucius Lucceius, as we saw, to write just such a pamphlet (not necessarily veracious) about his consulship.[22] In addition, according to Atticus, Cicero was not entirely truthful in his politically charged historical epic about Marius.[23] Caesar exaggerated the intransigence of his political enemy Pompey.[24]

Sallust spent a lot of time thinking about politics, being against the *nobiles* but by no means a *popularis*. His political attitude was complicated: although he was certainly not hostile to senatorial tradition, he believed that it had declined and that the decline of Rome resulted from this.[25] He chose the Jugurthine War because he saw it as the 'first challenge to the arrogance of the nobility'.[26] But he did not, perhaps, sufficiently appreciate that his contrast between conservatives and radicals, creating a two-party system, was too sharp; besides, the pattern continually changed.

Under the Roman principate the political picture had, of course, become quite different. Livy looked backwards to adopt an idealised, romanticised tradition of a harmonious senate, and disliked the *populares* of the third and second centuries BC (starting with Gaius Flaminius and Gaius Terentius Varro).[27] Nevertheless, he had to appreciate that Augustus was now in charge, and showed prudence about this question, even if the view that he became a propagandist for the new regime is now out of favour.[28]

Tacitus was in two minds; he was a Republican at heart, sentimentally, but was aware that the principate was inevitable, and needed.[29] In other words, he ambiguously lacked a clear political philosophy, and he was aware, also, that passions among his readers ran high. Ammianus Marcellinus, too, had to be careful about politics, because he, a pagan, was writing under the Christian emperor Theodosius I. Thus, he was over-partial, for political reasons, to Theodosius's father of the same name.[30] His own political views were somewhat mixed. He hated the upper classes, who, he thought, had failed Rome and who had cold-shouldered him there. But he also felt, as we have seen, a great dislike for the proletariat.

Anachronism

Whether modern or ancient, historians cannot escape the times in which they live; it is futile for them to attempt to do so.[31] They are 'the autobiographers of their generation': every age must rewrite history in its own way. To say, as Lord Acton did, that 'only a foolish liberal judges the past with the ideas of the present', is to demand the impossible: historians cannot help being influenced by the present in which they live,[32] although they would be wise not to engage in 'relentless modernising', as did Mommsen and Meyer, for example, who were always conscious of their own nineteenth-century Germany.[33] The Greek and Roman historians, whether consciously or unconsciously, were equally affected by the times to which they belonged. Moreover, other factors which inevitably intruded themselves (and once again this is equally true of the historians' modern counterparts)[34] were their own personalities and tastes, their outlooks and attitudes.

This was evident from the very beginning. Herodotus was strongly influenced by contemporary events, and viewed the Persian Wars through the distorted lens of his own time, committing anachronisms as a result.[35] Thucydides did not adequately grasp the concept of time or historical perspective, and his Funeral Speech of Pericles, for example, displays a retrospective nostalgic idealism,[36] although the age of which he is advanced as the representative had been exceedingly different from the age in which Thucydides himself was writing.

Polybius practically made a virtue of political anachronism, attaching special value to the 'ability to draw analogies between parallel circumstances of the past and of our own times'. This gives us, he maintained, a basis for deductions and inferences about the future.

> It is the mental transference of similar circumstances to our own times that give us the means of forming presentiments of what is about to happen, and enables us at certain times to take precautions and at others by reproducing future conditions to face with more confidence the difficulties that menace us.[37]

As for all of the historians of Rome who followed, they were, without exception, profoundly and inescapably enmeshed in the epochs and political ambiences in which they lived. Thus, Sallust's long denunciation of Sulla flagrantly bears on the contemporary political situation[38] (and he was a man who saw his own unhappy experiences as mirroring the political troubles of Rome).[39] When we pass on to Livy

> a large part of his detailed narrative of the various episodes is strongly coloured with overtones of the political battles of the late Republic. . . . Much of Livy's language and setting is coloured by the struggles of the post-Gracchan era.[40]

Plutarch, too, was anachronistic, because he did not appreciate the political changes that history brought about.[41] Tacitus, as we saw, was deeply divided, if not schizophrenic, about his theoretical adherence to the old Republic and his practical appreciation that the principate was inevitable and, if the rulers were good enough, even desirable. Besides failing on occasion to take time or circumstances into account, and being imperfectly informed about Republican affairs, Tacitus sometimes (no doubt inevitably) projects into the past the preoccupations, the affairs of his own day.[42]

CHAUVINISM

Athens and Rome

While it is natural that authors should express undue favour to their own country or to the country that has adopted them, it is bad for history.[1] It is a practice which is often seen today, and which affected Greek and Roman historians very gravely, especially after the development, in the fifth century BC, of monographs studying and praising individual cities and peoples. Lucian understandably remarked that 'statelessness' was the best thing for a historian.[2] Another good thing – or often the same thing – was banishment; it is useful that quite a number of the greatest historians were removed from their own cities or countries.

> It has repeatedly been noticed that historians were often voluntarily or compulsorily exiles from their own city. . . . This may even suggest that historiography, unless it was local history written to satisfy local patriotism, had an ambiguous status in Greek society. It was certainly easier to get proper information for a large subject, and to be impartial, if one had the mobility of an exile.[3]

Herodotus contrasted Greeks and non-Greeks, and was thus partly responsible, following Homer, for the age-long gulf fixed between east and west.[4] Yet he set it as his aim to record the 'mighty and wonderful deeds of the Greeks *and barbarians*', and he avoided being anti-Persian, maintaining a remarkable degree of objectivity in the matter, based partly on his employment of good sources relating to Persia.[5] On the other hand Herodotus displayed excessive favour to Athens which had admitted him, and which repaid his efforts with large rewards. He declared, exaggeratedly, that it was the Athenians who had been the principal victors of the Persian War: whereas it could be argued that Sparta had been equally heroic.[6] (Plutarch, who reminded his readers that this was so, also declared that Herodotus was biased against the Boeotians and Corinthians.)[7]

Thucydides, on the other hand, whom Athens had exiled, probably overstated its unpopularity,[8] and was accused of being too kind to the Spartans.[9] Much more serious, however, was his extreme underestimate of the part played by Persia in ending the Peloponnesian War.[10] Reading his history, one would fail to appreciate that Persian intervention on the Spartan side had been decisive in the war. This omission arose from Panhellenic feelings which preferred to accept the idea that the warfare had been a wholly Greek affair, settled by Greeks.

Xenophon, although like Herodotus he did not share Greek prejudices against barbarians,[11] underplayed events in Greece itself, including Persian interventions, that had taken place outside the

Spartan sphere (even if his enthusiasm for Sparta waned).[12] He was poorly informed, or insufficiently informative, about the Athens from which he had become estranged. Thus, his information was extremely inadequate, indeed glaringly inefficient, with regard to the formation of the Second Athenian Confederacy. He hated Thebes, and had nothing to say about the foundation by the Thebans of the Arcadian city of Megalopolis (370–362 BC), which was often hard pressed by Sparta.[13]

It was regrettable that, not long afterwards, Plato felt able to coin the term 'noble lies', indicating that some falsehoods were necessary to cover patriotic purposes:[14] this became, of course, a justification for many chauvinisms.

Polybius quite definitely, for his own patriotic reasons, supported some Greeks, notably the Achaean League (in which his father Lycortas had held high office) and (semi-Greek) Macedonia, while similar motives caused him to attack others:

> His patriotic bias certainly leads him to neglect the rule of impartiality when he is dealing with states hostile to his own country. His hatred of Aetolia and the Aetolians is too patent to need illustration.... His hostile picture of the career of Cleomenes [III] of Sparta ... goes back to the *Memoirs* of Aratus.... Political prejudice has also deformed his picture of conditions in third-century Boeotia.... Polybius allows his assessment of a situation to be coloured by the attitude of those concerned in it towards Achaea or Rome.[15]

Indeed, while aware of the dangers of chauvinism, Polybius openly conceded the historian's right to set an example by exhibiting patriotic bias, though he would not admit to the employment of lies in order to do so. But this made him wrong, for example, not only about Boeotia (inscriptions tend to show it had not declined), but also about Aetolia, concerning which an inscription can be used against him. One of the reasons why he disliked, again, his predecessors (p. 42) was because they had criticised his friends.[16]

Yet Rome, to which Polybius and other Achaeans had been forcibly taken, was never condemned by Polybius as an aggressor, although he was writing for Greeks; he shows curious ambivalences and discrepancies about Roman policy.[17] But, in his support of Greeks and Romans alike, he was basically pro-western: he saw fundamental differences between westerners and eastern barbarians,[18] and he regarded Carthage as the instigator of the Second Punic War.[19]

Sallust was a standard, fraudulent eulogiser of early Rome.[20] So, too, was Livy, whose frank intention (while withholding personal belief or disbelief) was 'to glorify Rome, to flatter national vanity, and to inspire in Roman youth patriotic ardour and affection'[21] – affection, that is, for senate, army, and leaders. This involved considerable distortions.[22] For example, his account of Coriolanus is a complete invention. It is part of his presentation of early Rome in terms of an over-simplified, idealised Roman character, which had really never existed.[23] Nor does he ever admit the early Etruscan domination of Rome.

Livy, indirectly, justified such distortions by his admiration of the city in the early days of its life.

> I hope my passion for Rome's past has not impaired my judgement. For I do honestly believe that no country has ever been greater than ours or richer in good citizens and noble deeds; none has been free for so many generations from the vices of avarice and luxury; nowhere have thrift and plain living been for so long held in such esteem. Indeed, poverty, with us, went hand in hand with contentment.[24]

It was unfortunate, however, that Livy extended these distortions down to historical times. He misdates the fall of Saguntum to 218 BC, instead of 219, thereby palliating (or accepting a source which palliates) the Roman failure to come to its help.[25] He leaves Rome innocent of war-guilt for the Second Punic War,[26] being weak on Carthage because of his blind patriotism in favour of its Roman opponents.[27] He is also at fault over the terms imposed on the Carthaginians by the Romans after the war was over.

If we compare Livy's account of the peace-terms imposed on Carthage after the Hannibalic War with those in Polybius, we find a general correspondence except on two issues. Livy says that Carthage was to make a *foedus* [treaty] with Masinissa [the king of Numidia] about their common boundary. Polybius does not mention this, and indeed such permissiveness on Rome's part would have been a remarkable departure from her diplomatic techniques. Secondly, Livy maintains that Carthage could not wage even defensive war in Africa under the treaty; these alleged clauses, which probably never existed, allowed Livy's sources more comfortably to assign responsibility for the Third Punic War to Carthage, when that city retaliated against constant Numidian retaliation. Many other examples of such problems in Livy's account caused by such chauvinistic distortions could be cited.[28]

For example, Livy is too pro-Roman about the Second Macedonian War (200–196) and he is too favourable to Titus Quinctius Flamininus, who brought it to an end with a Roman victory.[29] When Pollio accuses him of *Patavinitas*, provincialism because he came from the distant town of Patavium, one wonders whether he is not charging him with the blind Roman patriotism of a naïve frontiersman.[30]

Josephus, on the other hand, was a determined Jewish chauvinist. He almost outdid the Old Testament in exaggerating ancient Jewish power and strength and importance,[31] in deliberate contrast to the anti-Jewish slanders which had characterised Seleucid and subsequent literature.[32] *Deuteronomy* had told how the Jews were ordered to remember the past, and Josephus fell in determinedly with this intention, abandoning any claim to objectivity by his description of those who disagreed with his ideas as 'factious', 'tyrants', 'brigands' and 'malefactors'. (As for the First Jewish Revolt (AD 66–70), we should be in a better position to judge what he reports about it if we had not suffered the loss of Tacitus's account, which prevents us from offering a check.)[33]

Plutarch, as we said, accused Herodotus of being too sympathetic towards the barbarians. He also charged him with excessive partiality to Athens.[34] Yet he himself, a Greek, was eager that Athens should rival Rome and was always ready to try to point out that great Greeks were equal to great Romans.[35] In fact, he was a patriotic Greek (Oliver Goldsmith declared that one of his virtues was to give his readers a love of patriotism) and this did deprive him, at times, of impartiality. But he was more or less lacking in Greek vanity, and well aware that the Romans were the rulers.[36] What he felt, surely, was that, whereas the Romans were the rulers, the Greeks could provide the education that they needed in order to rule.

Tacitus was prevented from being totally objective about races because he disliked the Greeks very much.[37] But he did modify the traditional picture of westerners versus barbarians by his emphasis, in the *Germania*, on 'the noble savage', the 'unspoiled barbarian'. The theme was not altogether new,[38] but Tacitus devoted new force and eloquence to its development. Nevertheless, he was happy enough when the barbarians were defeated. Later on, Ammianus Marcellinus, although he never studied the Germans closely, and never called the Persians 'barbarians' (implying, by such avoidance, their equality to Rome[39]), held the eternal city in high admiration, as 'most sacred', essentially symbolic.

Beyond Athens and Rome

The strong tendency to chauvinism among ancient historians means that we hear too much about Athens and Rome, and not enough about other places. This applies, as far as Athens is concerned, to almost all Greek literature, which tells us far too little about the whole of the Greek world outside that leading city. We are, however, saved from the worst effects of this peril by the careers of the four leading historians. Herodotus came from far away, which meant that, although he settled in Athens and praised it, he remained aware of other Greek lands. Thucydides, as we saw, spent a great deal of his life exiled from Athens, with the result that he found himself closer to other centres. Polybius was transported from Greece to Italy, so that he, too, was forcibly detached from his homeland, although he remained emotionally close to it. Nevertheless, in spite of these peculiar circumstances, the great Greek historians do tell us far less than modern historians require about what was going on outside Athens.

When we come to the Roman historians, the situation becomes worse. Roman historians, as a rule, dealt only with the affairs of cities and states when they became relevant to Rome.[40] Tacitus begins his great work with the words *urbem Romam*, the city of Rome.[41] It was, after all, the centre of power and of a senator's interest and of the court scandals which principally interested the Roman public.[42] As a result, Tacitus tends to ignore the rest of the empire. Such 'neglect' has been defended, on the grounds that the history of the provinces was not part of his task,[43] but he could have said more about them, all the same. He did, in his *Germania*, say a lot about the Germans – not all of it without a moral purpose – and that was probably why Ammianus Marcellinus was negligent about them, because he did not want to rival Tacitus.[44]

The powerful tendency among ancient historians to concentrate on Athens and then Rome meant that they were often weak about the geography, topography and ethnography of other regions.[45] Some of them knew it: notably Herodotus, who wrote:

> About the far west of Europe I have no definite information. . . . In spite of my efforts to do so, I have never found anyone who could give me first-hand information about the existence of a sea beyond Europe to the north and west.[46]

But he is also disappointing about regions much nearer home, notably the lands of the Greeks themselves. Perhaps convention required him to be, since he had become, above all, an Athenian historian. Nevertheless, his un-Athenian background and wide travels gave him an outlook which was less centred upon Athens than those of many who wrote for its people. He saw no clear distinction between history and geography, both of which plainly play their part in human affairs. Indeed, some have believed that he himself was a geographer before he became a historian.

Thucydides, when he criticised his predecessors,[47] probably did not think much of their geographical knowledge. But he himself was desperately wrong about the topography of Pylos and Sphacteria.[48] Xenophon understood the employment of weapons and mechanical devices. Polybius professed an interest in warfare, of which he saw the importance to history (even when distant areas were concerned),[49] but, although he criticised Timaeus for inadequacy in this field,[50] his own geography was weak.[51] He says very little about Asia, and not much, it would seem, about Spain either. Here his epitomators may have been at fault.[52] Unfortunately, however, there is more to it than that, since Polybius undoubtedly made mistakes about Italy, and his Alpine locations are vulnerable.[53]

As for the Romans, they did not always choose to mention the geographical information that they probably possessed. Cicero urged historians to offer more extensive territorial descriptions,[54] but these were a speciality of rhetoricians of which not every historian could make use, and when they did, encouraged by Cicero's attitude, they sometimes perpetrated inaccuracies or inventions.[55] Caesar provided much useful information about the countries he visited, embarking, for example, on geographical excursions in the *Gallic War*.[56] But Sallust was impressionistically weak on geography. So was Livy, who 'adds purely fictitious detail which he remembered from his days at school when he would have been taught the basic techniques of how to describe landscapes'.[57] Thus, he was confused about Hannibal's Alpine route into Italy, embellishing his account by pure fiction.[58]

When we turn to areas further afield, Strabo pronounced that most writers about India are liars (*pseudologoi*).[59] The *Agricola* of Tacitus contains only eleven place-names, which is an indication of how vague his British geography was.[60] Equally vague was his geography of other places, including Armenia,[61] and in his battle-pieces he neglects topographical factors.[62] He understood the provinces quite well, but they and their configuration did not fit his concept of history or his method of writing.[63] Ammianus Marcellinus's memory of the topography of Amida is wrong in almost every respect.[64]

WARS

As we have seen, the preoccupation of the ancient historians with politics meant that they were also preoccupied with wars, and this has lasted as a main central historical theme. Long ago, I wrote a book to complain about it: after all, even if war is a natural or inevitable condition, there are many other interesting things that happen, and wars are not needed to produce necessary changes. Yet it remains undoubtedly true that, in pursuance of the theme of Homer's *Iliad*, war is 'the subject to which most historians in the ancient world devoted their attention'.[1]

It is unfortunate, therefore, that they were often inadequate about the causes of wars, and also that their descriptions of what went on during wars and battles were often conventional: it was a disputed question whether one had to have personal experience of them to write about them. What is clear, however, is that it is very hard to discover what actually happened when a battle was going on.[2] Tolstoy's *War and Peace* showed how different military confrontations look from the viewpoint of a general and a soldier, who can rarely see anything of the pattern of a battle in which he is engaged, and General Sir Ian Hamilton remarked on a strong tendency to self-glorification after battles.[3] One might add that it is usually the winner who writes about them, which is a further cause of distortion. Speeches by generals to the troops (pp. 44–53) cannot possibly be authentic.[4]

Herodotus, although he saw the 'memorable deeds of men' as mainly military (so that he was largely responsible for the war theme of European history) and although he gathered information about such engagements where he could get it, did not possess the most elementary knowledge of warfare and is very bad about the numbers of those who engaged in it.[5] He could describe military equipment, but he was at sea over tactics and was one of those who did not think logically about causes.

Thucydides, who was determined to point out that the Peloponnesian War was the greatest war of all time,[6] perpetuated, with repercussions upon many of his successors, the emphasis on military operations (which he describes without the customary one-sidedness and malice).[7] He displayed, also, the inadequacy of ancient information about the causes of wars. Indeed, it seems to us extraordinary that he excludes the Megarian Decrees from the causes of the Peloponnesian War.

No modern historian, probably, would have omitted to note the *psephisma* of Charinus, which followed up the decrees excluding Megara from the markets of Athens and her empire, by excluding Megarians on penalty of death from the very soil of Attica.

Thucydides would have said that it did not affect the outbreak of the war.[8]

We believe that he was wrong. Nevertheless, his descriptions of battles were good.

Xenophon was keen enough on giving military instruction,[9] even if it remained for contemporary specialists to add the professional touch which he could not claim.[10] Polybius took the view that it was essential for the historian to have some experience of war if he was going to write about it.[11] He himself, fortified as he believed by this experience, had a passion for describing warfare, though his idea of historical causes is rather crude and dogmatic.[12]

Sallust, too, is unreliable about the causes of the Jugurthine War, and his accounts of battles are bad on numbers, dates, locations and distances, and are generally patchy, uneven and capricious.[13] His defence against such charges was that battles *are* chaotic and chancy.

As to causes of wars, Cicero makes the orator Marcus Antonius offer a very strict analysis: that history demands 'an exposition of all contributory causes, whether originating in accident, discretion or foolhardiness'.[14] Caesar is, of course, somewhat suspect on this matter, because he is so anxious to point out that neither the Gallic War nor the Civil War was his fault. But he offers very clear descriptions of all military activities, since he was writing for his own class who valued military success so highly.[15]

Livy, although his panoramic study assumed a mainly military character and he stressed the military skills that helped to create the Roman empire,[16] was deplorably bad and uninformed (or, at best, imaginative) about wars and battles and military matters in general.

> The parts of his history left to us are in large measure concerned with commanders and their armies. How unfortunate, therefore, that he had not the mind of a Xenophon! Equally unfortunate was his lack of military experience which made him ignorant of battle tactics. . . .
>
> But it is in siege descriptions that the clearest picture emerges of a mind wholly indifferent to the technique of war . . . Livy scrutinises his sources without the insight of a military expert. . . . His indifference to the finer points of soldiering, and his awareness of a non-specialist audience, make him aim at a comprehensive and stimulating account. . . . Mistakes [are] caused by inexperience, obscurity, omission of vital detail, over-dramatisation, or oversimplification.[17]

As a result, since he is writing for non-specialists, Livy not only invents (and stereotypes) earlier warfare (his north Italian wars show 'the usual annalistic compound of fictitious detail and contamination')[18] but he also gravely distorts the battles that took place early in the Second Punic War. Indeed, his battle pictures are for the most part total inventions. He often reuses old accounts, imitating what he himself has written. And, as we have seen (pp. 72–3), he carefully shifts war-guilt for the Second Punic War away from the Romans. Moreover, he never attempts to explain why Rome won the war in the end. His picture of the battle of Lake Trasimene is brilliant, but wholly fictitious.

> When we read this passage (and many others like it) our instinctive response to it is a literary one and not a historical one in our sense of the word. What I mean is that we do

not concern ourselves with the details of the event: we do not, that is, start noting down the facts. . . . We are struck, rather, by the power of the writing; we are impressed by the way in which the atmosphere, the 'feel' of the situation, is conveyed. . . .

Now and then, almost as though he cannot help himself, the narrator speaks in the present tense, and in the one word *cerneres*, 'you could have seen', he pulls the reader almost literally into what is happening. . . . Livy's account is presumably wholly imaginary.

But . . . to say that it is untrue is simply wrong. Its truth lies, not in its corresponding to 'what actually happened' . . . but in the fact that it convinces on the level of art, and thereby elevates the episode from the particular to the universal.[19]

(Of this theme of 'History as Literature', more will be said, see pp. 97–9).

Tacitus defined the fundamental quality of an emperor as military leadership. Yet he himself, in what he wrote, made many military mistakes. Like Livy, he reused battle stories that had served for earlier occasions, provided that they effectively displayed the 'varied incidents of battle'.[20] The war story in his *Agricola*, like some of his other accounts, does not agree with modern archaeology. His chronology is sometimes at fault.[21] His *Histories* 'viewed battles as psychological dramas',[22] neglecting strategy and tactics, so that Mommsen described him as 'the most unmilitary of historians'.[23] Nevertheless, he himself was determined to write about bloodshed, death, torture, heroism and sex – the traditional elements of sensational war literature. In the *Annals*, he is very weak on the campaigns of Germanicus,[24] and his account of Boudicca's British revolt is full of omissions, most of which are quite intentional, in the interests of brevity, speed and concentration.[25] Indeed, as he shows in his account of the confrontation between Caecina and Arminius, he is more interested in atmosphere than in facts.

What we respond to here is not the details of the episode as 'facts', but the overall 'feel' of the passage and the astonishing way in which Tacitus conveys the atmosphere of the occasion. . . . Tacitus . . . is providing us with a convincing account because from his own experience he can identify totally with what is happening.[26]

But that does not mean that he tells us what was really happening.

In the last resort, the war pictures of Tacitus are perhaps chiefly of value today because, although he is sometimes sceptical about non-military solutions,[27] he so often and sensibly sees military operations as futile, leading to no good effects. In this respect his accounts of warfare may be related to the assessment by Josephus of the First Jewish Revolt, which Josephus rightly saw as completely useless.[28] Battles have usually not been decisive even in the medium term, and this was appreciated by the best of the ancient historians, even when they took warfare as their principal theme.

BIOGRAPHY

The usual modern view is that the ancient Greek and Roman writers went too far in their emphasis on the lives of great men as the major components and constituents of history. True, we must not go too far in the opposite direction, as some Marxists have.

> Marx's doctrine allowed too small a role to powerful individuals. This is largely due to Engels's disastrous remark that 'Napoleon did not come by chance, and if he had not come another man would have taken his place.' This has caused many Marxists to belittle decisive men who, according to them, merely identified themselves with conditions independent of them. (Not all, however, have made this mistake: nor, without qualifications, did Marx himself)....
>
> The truth rather is that history is and usually has been directed by only a few men, good or bad, although those, of course, have their being within the framework of their community.... Clearly history would not have taken quite the turn it did if the peculiar personal characteristics of Napoleon or Augustus had not influenced it.[1]

Nor need we suppose that history, or ancient history, is entirely a matter of trends and tendencies, in which the role of the individual does not matter. We have been encouraged in this view by the existence of appalling dictators in our own century. Nevertheless, it must be admitted that, vitally important though leaders are, the ancients went too far in attributing every development to them, as though not only trends and tendencies but also the greater part of the population as well, did not exist.[2]

Besides, biography, modern or ancient, is flagrantly liable to abuse and irrelevancy, as Seneca the younger realised when he warned against undue hostility or favour (*nihil nec offensae nec gratiae dabitur*)[3]. Lucian, too, denounced fraudulent biography,[4] following Aristotle, who had pointed out the dangers of attempting too much psychological investigation and description.[5]

Herodotus, as always, set the pace when he (over-) stressed the whims of potentates as causes, and when he laid a great deal of Homeric emphasis upon the valour of individuals, whom he saw as the key to the universe. He includes in his writing a number of works of biography, which was just beginning to be recognised as an art. In general, he was preoccupied with great men and this sometimes led him into dubious history. It seems very doubtful, for example, whether the famous meeting between Solon and Croesus ever took place.[6]

Thucydides, too, overemphasised dominant personalities. He was interested in their minds; but his descriptions of the characters of individuals were not very impressive.[7] They were also highly imaginative, as we have seen already in his depiction of the thoughts of Nicias (p. 62). Xenophon was a pioneer experimenter in biographical forms, but produced greatly idealised portraits of the individuals who shaped events.[8] Although he was capable of distinguishing eulogy from history, his study of Cyrus in the *Cyropaedia* (*Education of Cyrus*) is ludicrously admiring, as is his hero-worshipping account of *Agesilaus* of Sparta. His homespun picture of Socrates in the *Memorabilia* never fails to inspire surprise, because it is so very different from Plato's version; but the one account is probably as unauthentic as the other.[9] Isocrates had developed the art of the encomium (with his *Euagoras*), and there was too normal an expectation that historiography and biography would have an encomiastic slant.[10] Polybius warned against extravagant praise (and, conversely, excessive vituperation, of which he considered that Timaeus was too lavish),[11] and contrasted panegyric with history. However, he stressed the importance of personality and character, and showed considerable psychological acumen, although his pioneer inclusion of exemplary actions as models of behaviour was perilous, and he himself was guilty of partisanship when he wrote about his Arcadian hero Philo-poemen.[12]

Nevertheless, Polybius very strongly asserted the view that the historian must take care to avoid favour or malice.

> When a man takes on the character of a historian, he must forget all such emotions; he will often have to praise and glorify his enemies in the highest terms, when their actions demand it, and often criticise and blame his dearest friends in harsh language, when the errors in their conduct indicate it.
>
> A living creature that has lost its eyes is entirely crippled. Equally, when truth is removed from history, the remainder turns out to be a useless tale. So one must not hesitate to arraign his friends or to compliment his enemies. Again, he must not shrink from blaming and then sometimes praising the same party, since it is impossible for people caught up in affairs to act rightly at all times and not probable that they should constantly be wrong.
>
> It is therefore our task, in our histories, to take a neutral stand as between the actors and to make our judgements and evaluations in accordance with the nature of the actions themselves.[13]

In the wake of a rash of apologetic Roman biographies and autobiographies (led by Sulla's), Cicero, deeply interested in the varied fortunes of prominent men and in the depiction of their characters, saw that the line between history and panegyric was fine and difficult to draw. Nevertheless, he determined to differentiate between them, insisting that a historian must not show partiality or hatred, and that mere inventions must be recognised.[14] However, as we saw (p. 64), his letter to Lucius Lucceius discloses the desire that his own consulship should be depicted in exaggeratedly favourable terms. It may also be repeated that Atticus maintained that Cicero had invented biographical facts in his epic poem *Marius*. Moreover, Cicero was also partly responsible for insistence, leading to over-insistence, on biographies of the great. History, he said, 'demands particulars of the lives and characters of such as are outstanding in renown and dignity'.

Sallust firmly placed individuals at the centre of the stage. His favour to Sertorius was extravagant; but he chose to neglect Cicero and his 'portrayal of Julius Caesar is pervaded by doubts and ambiguity'.[15]

If anyone excessively emphasised personalities, it was Livy. His heroes are lamentably insipid. Yet he sets out to build up history on a psychological basis, through the portrayal of emotions.[16] This increasing emphasis on the role of leading individuals had come to stay; it fitted in well with the imperial regime that had now been installed, since imperial history became and remained the history of the emperors.[17] They were 'outsize men' who accommodated the growing conviction that impersonal forces were not enough.[18] Thus, the main preoccupation of senatorial historians under the principate was the relationship between emperor and senate.[19] Josephus was therefore well aware that there were lies about the emperor Nero on both sides. He himself was a passionate hater of persons,[20] and also sometimes a staunch supporter: his emphasis on Titus's unwillingness to destroy the Jewish Temple at Jerusalem is probably quite untrue.[21]

Plutarch's analyses of character reveal an understanding of human feeling and motivation. Tacitus, so ambiguous, as we have seen, in his contradictory love for the Republic but awareness that the principate had to come, fastened upon the evil of rule by one man as his central theme – thus providing the most powerful ancient evocation of tyranny – and needed a villain to blame for this situation.[22] He found this villain in Tiberius, the prototype of Domitian under whom Tacitus had pursued his career, which later afflicted him with agonies of guilt. Or rather, the facts did not really tell against Tiberius, so Tacitus made up for them by innuendo. He described Tiberius unfairly, but treated Tiberius's mother Livia with even nastier unfairness.[23] Yet he did so with uncanny satirical skill, since, as Macaulay stated, 'he was unrivalled among historians in delineation of character', which he believed shaped events, when the characters were those of the leaders: so that Jerome called the *Annals* 'The Lives of the Caesars'.[24] Nevertheless, Tacitus claimed unswerving impartiality, well aware of the flatteries and animosities which prevented the composition of good history in an imperial age.[25] This, he said, was the result, as far as their writings were concerned:

> To an understandable ignorance of policy, which now lay outside public control, was in due course added a passion for flattery, or else a hatred of autocrats. Thus neither school bothered about posterity, for the one was bitterly alienated and the other deeply committed.

But whereas the reader can easily note the bias of the time-serving historian, detraction and spite find a ready audience. Adulation bears the ugly taint of subservience, but malice gives the false impression of being independent. . . .

Partiality and hatred towards any man are equally inappropriate in a writer who claims to be honest and reliable.

Yet Tacitus, for all his insight into human character,[26] did not really live up to this high standard. He displayed a certain tendency to adopt rhetorical stereotypes. One notices specific excesses. Quite apart from his unjust treatment of Tiberius and Livia, he gave too much prominence to the last extravagances of Messalina, who had little influence.[27] In addition, he overstressed Agrippina the younger (to whose memoirs he owed some of his hostile remarks about Tiberius), and Nero's second wife Poppaea. He also accepted too readily the unfriendly senatorial tradition about Claudius, representing him as a mere tool of others.[28] Conversely, his sustained, rather flat panegyrics of Germanicus and Corbulo are exaggerated or untruthful, as also had been his earlier praise of his stepfather Agricola.[29]

Suetonius was a biographer, and was thoroughly biographical. He did not, it is true, make a great effort to grasp whole personalities, but the people whom he describes – and 'it is the emphasis on the individual that makes him readable'[30] – are saturated with lust, brutality and perversion. However, at least he set down their supposed characteristics in a laid-back, apparently impartial manner, which is more than that other biographer Plutarch did. For Plutarch, while firmly establishing the principle that history is the product of the will and passion of individuals (so that biography has become the key to history,[31] although he realises that the two things are different),[32] was a hero-worshipper. He was interested in the images of great men[33] and in spreading their fame, and was ready to detect malice against them. He was poor on the development of character, however, and was sometimes rather insipid and not uninfluenced by imperial propaganda.[34] Nevertheless, he was well aware that there was not always enough evidence to assess a personality as carefully as one should.[35]

Ammianus Marcellinus, whose strongest point is characterisation, resulting in some acute surveys of personality, seems keen to avoid a partisan viewpoint about the individuals whom he describes,[36] but sometimes falls into the trap all the same. It must be repeated that he is over-partial to Julian and too kind to his own former commander Ursicinus.[37] He is also too favourable to Count Theodosius, the father of the ruling emperor Theodosius I, in order to avoid possible reprisals.[38] It was dangerous, in the later empire, to write too freely, although this was a time when biographies were abundant.

It would indeed have been hard for a historian and public servant living in such a perilous age to have achieved complete objectivity about everybody, and Ammianus does not do so.

For one thing, he paints an unmitigatedly black picture of Constantius II's nephew and deputy Constantius Gallus, who was struck down. Probably Gallus was cruel, perhaps monstrously so. But a more balanced picture would also have indicated his talents as a military commander, his popularity with the troops and proletariat, and the likelihood that, when he suppressed conspirators, at least some of them were guilty of the charges brought against them.[39]

MORALISING

We ought to be a little thoughtful before we condemn excessive moralising in the ancient historians,[1] because we ourselves, or many of us, have indulged in a good deal of moralisation in the present century. That is to say, in the great wars that have been fought and the great issues that have been raised, we have believed that we have been morally right and our enemies have been morally wrong. That is to say, we have assured ourselves that right and wrong exist and are real, and that we have been on the ethically correct side. In other words, we are not impartial about our own times, and do not believe that we should be.[2] 'The principles of true politics', declared Burke, 'are those of morality enlarged, and made without love and hate.'[3]

Morality is unavoidable in history, even if it is only implicit.[4] Are we, therefore, entitled to criticise the ancient historians of Greece and Rome because they took a similar line? Probably the answer is yes, because they carried the matter very far indeed. True, there is a case to be made for their not being content with history as a bare array of facts: some interpretation is essential, and that interpretation cannot help involving the injection of some judgement. The extent to which this is permissible has involved a considerable variety of opinions. One school of thought maintains that moralising is not the historian's main job; he or she should allow the facts to speak for themselves.[5] In keeping with this is the suggestion that the historian is entitled to pronounce judgements, but does so as moralist and not as historian.[6] But J. B. Bury was nearer reality when he remarked, 'I do not think that freedom from bias is possible, and I do not think it is desirable': impartiality, he maintained, was out of the question.[7]

The ancient writers were mostly convinced that this was so, and that it was their function to impose their opinions on their captive audience (literally captive, when they sat in the hall listening to what was said, and equally unable or unwilling to respond when they read what had been written). The historians felt this particularly strongly because they knew their kinship to tragedy, with which they were linked by a moral purpose (pp. 27–30).[8] True, some but not all Greeks prized detachment, but their Roman successors invariably seem to have regarded moral teaching as essential. All historians have prejudices and preconceptions and the ancients were not slow about displaying theirs.[9]

Herodotus has been attacked for moralising, but his morality (linked with religious ideas about overdoing things) is largely cautionary,[10] and so does not interfere too much. Thucydides was endeavouring to pursue truths about people's behaviour in war and politics, but he did not introduce moral standards in any too blatant a fashion, although he was not consistently cynical, and did not ally himself totally with the moral nihilism of the sophists.[11] Xenophon, on the other hand, went in a great deal for judgements,[12] although they are mostly of a somewhat commonplace character; his depiction of Agesilaus is profoundly moralistic and idealistic. The attribution to history of an entirely moralistic function went back to Isocrates (*Antidosis, Euagoras*), and by the end of the fourth century the subject had become openly judgemental.[13]

Polybius was unswervingly didactic and included exemplary actions as models of behaviour, saw history as a storehouse of examples of this kind, and declared adherence to a firm ethical standard.[14] This landed him in a certain amount of difficulty, because he tried to apply moral criteria to decisions which had really been reached on grounds of expediency.[15] Yet the way of life to which he adhered was not unpractical. Be moderate in prosperity, he said: because it will be remembered in your favour. And he implied that even imperial power was subject to an ethical criterion.[16]

These preoccupations reached their climax in Sallust, who invented a past replete with Roman virtues. He traced a moral decline through Roman history, measuring people against an ideal standard, and seeing events as extended *exempla* of philosophical, moral truths about public affairs – some of which are little better than vague or irrelevant generalisations.[17] Livy agreed with this view of Roman decline, and was greatly concerned with private virtue and public morality, of which he saw abundant examples and warnings in history.[18] In his preface Livy declares: 'I would like each person to give careful attention to the way of life, the values, the men, and the civil and military skills whereby this empire was acquired and extended.'[19]

> In other words, what is important for Livy, as he goes on to develop in the rest of the preface, is the moral and political function of history, in his case the task of reminding the Romans of their past greatness, in the hope of reversing their decline into greed and immorality, and inspiring them with a new and greater pride in themselves. . . . We can see him, if we like, as preaching a sermon.
>
> The work belongs to the strand of history aiming at moral education, though it follows an independent line. . . . A fact of history, the rise of Rome and her decline, was seen by Livy as a moral problem.[20]

Plutarch too, moralised quite explicitly (Goldsmith said that reading him will give the ruler a love of virtue) and he wrote his *Lives* in order to spell out and vindicate these ideals.[21]

Tacitus was equally convinced that history has an exemplary purpose: he had a powerful ethical aim. Indeed, his principles do not really take time or circumstances into account, and he has been declared a moralist rather than a historian.[22] He liked the idea that there were 'moral causes' behind the decline of the Roman government; thus his psychology is deeply moralistic, inculcating respect for honesty, and distaste for cruelty and tyranny.

ERROR

Another reason why the Greek and Roman historians fell short of modern standards of historiography was because they made mistakes. They got a number of their facts wrong. One must not, of course, be over-critical of this, because they were human and it is human to make mistakes. Besides, their sources were not as good as those which are available for modern scholars. Nevertheless, it remains true that the ancient historians did make mistakes and rather too many of them. Some of these mistakes were accidental, and are therefore cases of misinformation. Others are deliberate, and for deliberate reason, and are therefore disinformation.[1] 'Individual elements of the tradition were conflated, modified and sometimes invented.'[2]

Herodotus's mistakes were noted in Plutarch's treatise *On the Malice of Herodotus*.[3] Herodotus, of course, being so early, was very much hampered by the inadequacy of his information, and was conscious of this. He knew well that it was important that the evidence, such as it was, should be preserved, even if some of it was misleading.[4] It has been pointed out elsewhere that he gave altogether exaggerated figures for the Persian army which crossed the Hellespont in 480. And he often failed to make connections between events. However, K. J. Dover has also made the point that Herodotus and Thucydides sometimes went astray because they were pioneers (of genius), who had not yet formed the necessary conceptions which have subsequently been found essential for historiographers.[5]

Thucydides, apart from his weakness on the Megarian Decrees and the *psephisma* of Charinus and the importance of the Persian intervention in the Peloponnesian War (p. 77), was guilty of a good many errors and inadequacies, from which efforts to rescue him have failed.[6] He was, incidentally, handicapped by confusions between the solar and the lunar year.[7] Xenophon's *Hellenica*, which as we have seen ignores certain vital historical developments, contains numerous omissions, inaccuracies and fictions; and its cross-references are often obscure or completely absent.[8] Polybius, while aware of the dangers of ignorance, is sometimes too schematic, and offers discrepancies on Roman policy.[9] His chronology based on Olympic years was unfortunate, because it bisected campaigns.

Caesar was accused of inaccuracy by Gaius Asinius Pollio.[10]

Sallust, who deliberately misled in order to make a point and to achieve an effective composition, offered poor chronology, omission and abbreviation in the *Jugurtha*, and in the *Catiline* greatly magnified his villain.[11] The Catilinarian plot of 66–65, and the electoral contests ascribed to that year, may be wholly fictitious – erroneously antedating Catiline's revolutionary intentions. About the consular elections of 64, too, Sallust is distinctly obscure, and events in October and November 63 are presented with considerable inaccuracy. Nor is Sallust's information about politics, past or recent, always correct (p. 77). The 'message' from Publius Cornelius Lentulus to Titus Volturcius is an erroneous improvement on Cicero.[12]

It is by no means difficult to find mistakes in Livy:[13] factual errors, contradictions, idealising exaggerations, confusions in early plebeian history, constitutional vaguenesses (some of which can be blamed on his sources, which he reproduced too uncritically). The emperor Gaius (Caligula), ignoring Livy's beautiful style, regarded him as verbose and careless; a criticism echoed by Quintilian.[14] Like Sir Walter Scott, Livy wrote at a time in which there was widespread interest in the past, but not much learning. When Dante spoke of 'Livy who errs not', he was wrong.[15]

Tacitus declares himself well aware of the hindrances to the writing of history that were presented by ignorance, flattery and malice.[16] Nevertheless, he himself makes many mistakes.[17] In the *Histories*, he gets the Jews quite wrong, and echoes himself feebly about fratricide/patricide.[18] In the *Annals*, his mistelling of the British revolt is in the interests of a vivid composition,[19] and other stories are just romantic, fictitious bits of entertainment. The work begins with a particularly selective and inaccurate section; the passage about Germanicus's German campaigns is 'borrowed' from the *Histories* and earlier writers, and there are factual mistakes in the later books.[20] Indeed there are errors everywhere, even if they are not direct or intentional lies.

Such is the case, too, in Plutarch,[21] whose chronology is loose, vague or incorrect. He exaggerates, and commits many historical mistakes, and does not trace information back to its original source. Similarly, Suetonius's many sensational and bizarre anecdotes do not always bear a close relation to the truth.[22]

5

SHOULD WE READ THE ANCIENT HISTORIANS?

FACT AND FICTION

As I pointed out in the Introduction, the one thing that is certain about history is that what we are told is by no means always true. This is clearly perceptible today when we try to discover what is happening around us. We are encompassed on every side by inadequate information, distortions, inventions, falsifications and plain lies. The first of these unhappy situations, as was suggested in the last Chapter, may be described as misinformation, whereas the rest vary between misinformation and disinformation, having the deliberate intention of misleading people. The adepts in this practice have been the dictator states of the present century, which have set out to present to their public a picture that is often entirely false. Other governments, too, are by no means free from blame.

The same applies to many writers who have nothing to do with governments. Such writers have hopelessly blurred what ought to be an unarguable contrast between fact and fiction. The result of this blurring has been the creation of new terms. such as 'faction' – a blend of fact and fiction – and 'docudrama' and 'metahistory'.[1] These are all terms which imply, or indeed openly admit, that what is being said or written is not necessarily a historical fact but contains elements, perhaps dominant elements, of fiction. Well might Pontius Pilate say, as he allegedly did after listening to Christian protestations, 'What is truth?'[2] It is evident that we do not ever obtain the whole truth about what is happening today, and in consequence it is equally or even more evident that we do not, cannot, glean the whole truth about things that have happened in the past. 'I have tried to demonstrate', claimed R. Bruce-Lockhart, 'how impossible it is for history ever to be the truth,

90

the whole truth, and nothing but the truth.' Yet he adds that that is what we must aim at, all the same. 'It is the allotted task of historians always to seek it [the truth].'[3] As Jacques Barzun remarked,

> The public has picked up, somehow, at second-hand from the philosophers – or perhaps from Tolstoy or Stendhal – a radical scepticism about historical truth. There has been so much talk about 'metahistory', so much theorising about what the past is, how we know it, and who can possibly reconstruct it, that the intelligent layman is now proud of disbelieving: the record is crooked, the past has totally vanished – 'don't talk to me about history!'
>
> If one protests, the rejoinder comes pat: 'Look at all the revisionism. It has shown up one myth after another. History is politically motivated. Indeed, history is a weapon in the class struggle. Besides, it shows that every leader is a psychopath. History is amusing only when some of these heroes of old turn out pretty sorry specimens – and they had no influence on events anyway; forces do it all.'
>
> Sober history, no matter how artfully written, has no chance against such competition.[4]

Yet Bruce-Lockhart, as we saw, rightly adds that truth is what historians must aim at, nevertheless. It is their allotted task.

Yet their difficulty in doing so gives great point to Charles Dickens's observation, in *Our Mutual Friend*, that 'what to believe, in the course of his reading, was Mr Boffin's chief literary difficulty indeed'. This is particularly pointed because in Dickens's nineteenth century there arose a powerful conviction that history is a science, or can be raised or reduced to one. Lord Acton pronounced that 'ultimate' history was on the way, and was within reach.[5] Earlier, Ludwig von Ranke had asserted that history had to report only what had actually happened (*wie es eigentlich gewesen ist*).[6] There have been reams of literature about this saying, as indeed there have been about whether history can, or ought to, be described as a science. Ranke's definition is undoubtedly tempting. But perhaps one can leave all of the controversy aside, at least for the moment, and conclude that he is undoubtedly right about the need to be accurate about facts and events and their dates. There can be no dispute about whether a battle occurred, or a man died, in a certain year or on a certain day, although it is surprising how often even this sort of simple attribution can be stated erroneously or falsified.

Let us at least try, therefore, to get our facts right and in the right order at the right time and place; and to that extent at least we can subscribe wholeheartedly to Ranke's ruling. But then a much more difficult matter arises. The historian, even if he or she does have the facts right, will not be much good unless he or she makes some attempt to interpret them. Ranke's teacher Humboldt was well aware of this: he declared in 1821 that it is the duty of the historian to find out *the ideas behind the facts*.[7] The historian has 'to show why things happened and to discover the forces which were at work'.[8] It is his or her duty to note changes (explaining why they occurred), and relationships, causes and consequences, and to explain the sequence and connection of events.[9] There is, of course, a fundamental distinction between the data and the hypotheses that explain them,[10] but the historian has to tackle both. In doing so, he or she will come up against some weird and untenable theories, which must be rejected.

Nevertheless, apart from the necessity of getting the mere dates of events right, objectivity remains a vain dream. There are three reasons for this. First, the historian lives at a certain time and in a certain society, which he or she cannot fail to reflect by holding views which are inevitably conditioned by the mentalities and attitudes of his or her age and place.[11] 'Every generation', it has been said, 'must rewrite history in its own way.'[12] 'Every age has to rewrite its history, recreate the past; in every age a different Christ dies on the cross.'[13] This ought to be a good thing, because 'every historian ... has greater "historical experience" than his predecessors'.[14] It has not always worked out as a beneficial fact, however. It has meant, certainly, that 'the function of history is the elucidation of the present'.[15] But that can result in anachronisms when the past is being considered.

The second reason why historians cannot be objective is because they, personally, have their prejudices, their likes and dislikes.[16] They cannot escape their own personalities.[17] Whether they should even try to do so has been contested.[18] Anyway they cannot. Their own tastes are bound to intrude.[19] Or, as Theodor Mommsen put it, 'history is neither written nor made without love and hate.'[20] Herbert J. Muller made a similar statement at greater length.

Up to a point, all this implies something like Benedetto Croce's principle, that true history is always contemporary history – history . . . of what is alive for us. The past has no meaningful existence except as it exists for us, as it is given meaning by us . . . In our contemplation of the drama we see what is most pertinent for our own hopes and fears.[21]

'Clearly, the historian is present in his work with his whole personality.'[22]

This brings us to the third reason why historians are unable to be objective. Obviously, they have to select. There is no need to labour this point about the present time, when there is an indigestible mass of information, right or wrong, concerning every event.[23] But the same is equally true about past ages, when the information was less. This was discussed in pp. 42–4, but perhaps a little more might be added here, now that we are discussing objectivity. Selection is inevitably conditioned by something else as well: by ignorance. The historians cannot know everything, and have to select from what they do happen to know. But no one, as was rightly pointed out by Victoria Glendinning,

ever knows the whole story. . . . Inside the inside story are more stories. The people on the inside know a few small things, mostly about themselves. The people on the outside know a few big things, from which they draw wrong conclusions. So no one knows what's going on.[24]

However much argument may be generated by that, there is no doubt that the last sentence is true. 'Objectivity, even if achieved, was always confined within the narration of a chosen sequence of facts.'[25] And that means that objectivity is *not* achieved.

G. J. Renier is very good about all of this.

The action which is history is circumscribed, and limited to the accurate telling of an important and necessary story . . . Should the historian remain impartial when he tells his story? . . . Absence of bias is not the same thing as secure knowledge . . .

The historian's narrative cannot possibly be a faithful and total reproduction of a section of the past. But in our awareness of this limitation we still have to ask ourselves whether the historian is allowed to take sides, or whether he must keep his personality and preferences out of the story.[26]

Renier is attracted to a middle path, although he realises that it is painfully difficult to follow. Wilhelm Bauer explained 'that the cult of objectivity presents serious drawbacks, since its object can never be achieved.' He considers that the historian should avoid with equal care tendentiousness and colourless impartiality.'[27]

Another necessity which confronts historians today is that they should know something of social history, and include this in the pattern with which they confront their readers. This, too, has been discussed elsewhere (pp. 57–60), but here it must be added that the ancient failure to discuss social history sufficiently means another failure in objectivity.

Fact and fiction become pretty thoroughly mixed up today, and in the ancient world they were hopelessly mixed up and confused. It was widely recognised that historians did not, and could not be expected to, tell the truth. Either they preferred not to, because they wanted to publish biased views of their own, or they could not, because the truth was not accessible to them; perhaps it was no longer accessible to anybody. 'Ancient historians were not writing history as we know it.' And yet the claim to write truthfully and honestly and impartially was a standard cliché, which Seneca the younger parodies.[28] In fact, Lucian writes that it was the sole duty of the historian to do precisely this, 'to say exactly how things happened' (and this was perhaps the source of Ranke's famous saying to the same effect).[29]

Yet truth was often treated as if it were of secondary importance. It could even be suggested that there were two kinds of veracity, one actual, and the other a matter of outlook and attitude;[30] in other words, 'higher truth', unauthentic, though authentic enough as a story. In any case, 'the concept of history, in the objective sense, that is, as the aggregate of past events, was unknown to antiquity': in which people showed an inexhaustible ability to invent and to believe.[31] The boundary between truth and fiction was shifting and unsolid. Ancient readers, although their interests of course varied, did not, for the most part, expect a historian to avoid falsification altogether:[32] so that, if the writer sometimes shows disbelief in what he is reporting, this need cause no surprise. As will be stressed again later (pp. 97–9), the greatest ancient historians were mostly resplendent literary figures, who were closer to other literary genres than their modern counterparts. They intended to teach and also (in some cases) to entertain (not nowadays always admitted as a function of history), but they were, it must be repeated, *literary* personalities and 'it is virtually axiomatic that one cannot accept a literary source at its face value'.[33] Nor were these ancient historians expected to conduct much research;[34] some of them did indeed refrain from doing so. 'A mind like a mirror' was, instead, what they needed, according to Lucian:[35] displaying the shape of things just as they receive them'. But that was an ideal rarely or never achieved, because, as we saw, the facts needed interpretation, and interpretation inevitably brought in departures from factual truth.

> It would be hard to think of any historical writer in antiquity who does not, either explicitly or implicitly, allow himself to go beyond the established facts of a situation and indulge in imaginative reconstruction of one kind or another.[36]

There is, we are told, a widespread feeling that ancient authors are somehow privileged, exempt from the normal canons of evaluation.[37] But they ought not to be when it is a question of arriving at the truth, not the 'higher truth' but the truth of how things actually happened.

Herodotus led the way by incorporating in his *History* a great many stories that are most unlikely to be true, a fact of which he was perfectly well aware. He maintained that the decision to believe or disbelieve them rested with his readers, but he ambivalently continued to include such tales, as a modern historian would not.[38]

Thucydides was well aware of the necessity and difficulty of acquiring the truth, warning against 'reliance upon the exaggerated embellishments of the poets' (p. 26), but the orderliness which he himself imposes upon history is a product of his own powerful intellect, after the image of his own mind. Although he believed strongly in the utility of history (and it was he who invented Lucian's concept of the mirror, into which the historian's readers are invited to look),[39] the pictures which he presents, upon which this stamp has been imposed, are not as scientific as he thinks. Very often they are more than dubious, from the viewpoint of objective truth.[40]

Xenophon writes as a reporter, not as a historian.[41] He should be judged as a reporter or as an inventor of fiction, since that is what his *Education of Cyrus* is, and so investigations into his historical truthfulness are scarcely needed. Aristotle, however, saw research into historical facts as a necessary condition of the complete knowledge of human society: though he does not give history full scientific status, seeing science as the knowledge of the universal, and history of the particular.[42] It was in his time that *historia* became 'history',[43] though the exploits of Alexander the Great gave a vast stimulus to historical romance, and henceforward the overwhelming preoccupation of Hellenistic history was a desire to charm, divert and edify.[44]

It was Polybius above all others who saw history as didactic. Certainly, he insisted on the truth, provided that it was rightly interpreted.[45] But the reason why he insisted on it was to ensure that people, and especially politicians, should be quite clear, from the knowledge of the past, about what they should do and refrain from doing. He was also sometimes emotional,[46] although he would not have liked to admit it. However, he continues to stress the utility of history, and the careful investigations that it requires.

> Neither the writers nor the readers of history should concentrate so much on the narrative of the actual deeds as on what precedes, accompanies and follows each event. For if one removes from history a consideration of the causes, manner and reasons for the doing of each deed, and consideration of whether the result was what we should have expected, what is left of it turns out to be a fine composition but not a work of instruction.
>
> And, though entertaining for the moment, it will offer no utility whatever for the future.[47]

Cicero, or his spokesman Antonius, pronounced that the historian must tell the whole truth, and not be swayed by partiality or hatred – he disbelieved most of the early stories about Rome – and that the merits of outcomes should be assessed. However, he did add that an attractive style and some embellishment were needed,[48] and, as we saw, he was not above urging Lucceius to go beyond the truth where Cicero's own consulship was concerned.

Sallust complained that history is not easy: 'I regard the writing of history as one of the most difficult of tasks; first, because the style and diction must be equal to the deeds recorded.'[49] This emphasis on style, reminding us that history was primarily seen as a part of literature (pp. 97–9), is a little ominous, because it means that Sallust feels freer than one would have hoped to play fast and loose with the facts, in order to display, even more than he should, his 'flair for hypocrisy and fraudulence'. Livy allows himself Ciceronian echoes,[50] and is well aware that many of his stories about early times may well have no historical foundation:

> Events before Rome was born or thought of have come to us in old tales with more of the charm of poetry than of a sound historical record, and such traditions I propose neither to affirm nor to refute.
>
> There is no reason, I feel, to object when antiquity draws no hard line between the human and the supernatural. It adds dignity to the past, and, if any nation deserves the privilege of claiming a divine ancestry, that nation is our own.[51]

Thus Livy, unlike a historian of today, does not mind that many of his stories about archaic epochs are purely fictitious. Plutarch likewise insisted that the historian should display emotion, and should provide dramatic characters, although he was not at ease with what seemed to him to be the moral romanticism of Herodotus.[52]

Tacitus, too, although he seeks urgently to understand and interpret the events that he narrates, tells many tall stories, sometimes infused with his own black, savage humour.[53] He wrote with passion, and Collingwood declared: 'It is permissible to wonder whether he was a historian at all.'[54] Suetonius, on the other hand, is passionlessly indiscriminate, although this does not always make him fair. And Ammianus Marcellinus's literary tricks sometimes produce impressions which are not really compatible with truthfulness.

Nor, or course, are the Old Testament and New Testament always truthful, for history is not their primary purpose.

LITERARY EXCELLENCE

The main reason why we should read the ancient historians is not because they were great historians (which, by modern standards, they could not be expected to be) but because they were literary artists. Some of them were of altogether outstanding quality. Historians intended, and desired, to please; and their readers, or listeners, wanted to be pleased.[1] There was a strong tendency, therefore, to convert history into historical romance.[2]

My assertion that, by modern standards, these ancient writers were not great historians has been illustrated in the foregoing pages. It does not by any means signify, however, that in our search for information about the ancient world we should neglect them. Despite all their shortcomings, they are still by far our best single source of information about Greece and Rome.[3] But they do not tell us enough, and some of what they tell us is wrong. We have to accept the fact that they remain somewhat different from their modern counterparts. Besides, what they present to us relates to epochs that existed a very long time ago. In all likelihood, we should not expect to learn from them as much about those epochs as we do about modern periods. That is precisely what makes the task of today's historians, attempting to reconstruct ancient Greece and Rome, so interesting. There is no need to repeat here all of the arguments in favour of our learning about the classical world.[4] We ought to learn about it, and yet the task of doing so is difficult, and must be recognised as such. Let us look, therefore, as clearly and honestly as we can at the great historians of the ancient world and let us conclude, from our earlier researches, just what they have to offer, and what warnings should be presented about what they do not offer.

Some of them were magnificent literary artists. (Even those who were not have set their stamp, in one way or another, upon subsequent ages.) This makes them worthy of careful consideration.

> Ancient and modern historiography are two quite different things. . . . What we ought to be doing is approaching ancient historians as the writers of literature which they are. They should be compared with Latin poets . . . or with modern reporters or creative writers. . . . Our primary response to the texts of the ancient historians should be literary rather than historical since the nature of the texts themselves is literary.
>
> Only when literary analysis has been carried out can we begin to use these texts as evidence for history.[5]

> What we are talking about . . . is (on one level) literary or artistic truth. The accounts may nor be historically true in

98

our sense of the word – that is, they may not be an accurate account of what actually happened – but that is not the point. What matters is that they *ring* true, they *feel* right, they are convincing.

On this level, perhaps, it is enough simply to emphasise . . . the literary nature of Greek and Roman historical writing, the fact that historiography in antiquity is a literary genre . . . judged by literary criteria . . . Literary truth, for history as well as tragedy, is a valid and entirely respectable aim.[6]

The glory of the ancient historians is unrelated to any particular age, because it is timeless. We must read them because of the wonderful and influential literature that they wrote.

To sum up, it is necessary to repeat, once again, that ancient history was understood not as history, according to our meaning of the word, but as literature. There is no doubt that this is detrimental to their value as historians. 'Brilliant and ingenious writing has been the bane of history: it has degraded its purpose, and perverted many of its uses.'[7] Above all, it has provided the opportunity for a great deal of misinformation. When Lytton Strachey declared that 'the first duty of a great historian is to be an artist' he was, in a sense, echoing Lucian's belief that a good historian must have 'powers of expression'.[8] He was also opening the way to this ruination of history as an activity in its own right,[9] and Mommsen was not far wrong when he classified historians among artists rather than scholars, believing that it was artists that they had to be.[10] 'A writer was not called a historian unless he had considerable pretensions to style.[11] A historian had to entertain, and for that purpose he did not need truth as much as wit.[12] This became more and more evident. 'In the end, the demands of artistry gained precedence over those of science.'[13]

OTHER SOURCES OF
INFORMATION

OTHER HISTORIANS

This book has been largely concerned with the principal historians whose works have survived, but there were many others as well, whose writings are extant, at least in large part, but who do not deserve to figure among those who led the historical movements of the successive ages.

First of all, mention should be made of three who wrote in Greek.

The 'Old Oligarch'

The 'Constitution of Athens' was not by Xenophon, among whose works it was included. Its author is described as the 'Old Oligarch'.

> He was the most bone-headed kind of conservative, anti-democratic, anti-Athenian, and violent against slaves and the poor. . . .
> He is hardly able to string a sentence together. His style is amusingly simple, but not genuinely archaic.
> This buffoon is highly valued by scholars as a witness and a rare example of the opposition to the Periclean party, and of pristine, pre-sophistic prose. . . . My own view is that the author was some minor member of the circle of the Four Hundred, writing between 413 and 411 to promote sedition overseas.[1]

As for the periods of Greek literary history that followed, 'the tenuous surviving material of the fourth and third centuries suggest that the standards [of Thucydides] were largely abandoned.'[2]

Diodorus Siculus

Diodorus Siculus, from Agyrium in Sicily, wrote, from c. 60–30 BC, a *World History* in massive dimensions. The work itself is undistinguished, superficial and unoriginal.[3] Diodorus modestly disclaims deep insight, and is not afraid to use second-hand material; his *History* is valuable to us because of these authorities whom it quotes. Correctly maintaining that some histories are, to an excessive extent, 'appendages to oratory', he nevertheless pronounces that it is legitimate for writers to display rhetorical prowess, 'since history needs to be adorned with variety'.[4] However, he writes strongly against the inclusion of frequent speeches (pp. 44–54), even though he adds an indulgent word about those who like to invent them. On this subject of speeches Diodorus had some interesting observations to make.

> One might justly censure those who in their histories insert overlong orations or employ frequent speeches. For not only do they rend asunder the continuity of the narrative by the ill-timed insertion of speeches, but they also interrupt the interest of those who are eagerly pressing on toward a full knowledge of events.
>
> Yet surely there is opportunity for those who wish to display rhetorical prowess to compose by themselves public discourses and speeches for ambassadors, likewise orations of praise and blame and the like.[5]

Dionysius of Halicarnassus

Dionysius of Halicarnassus lived and gave instruction at Rome for a long time, from 30 BC onwards. In addition to numerous rhetorical writings and other essays and letters, he wrote the *Roman Antiquities*, of which, out of twenty books, ten survive.

It is a moralising history ('philosophy teaching by example'), and a panegyric of Rome, whose empire seemed to him the culmination of world history. Dionysius devoted careful research to the work.[6] He believed that history needed great subjects, and good men[7] – and was not unwilling to compare Greeks and Romans,

101

whose rule he saw as permitting a Greek Renaissance.[8] He was not afraid of assuming that Rome had become Hellenised from an early date. He was well aware of the implications of selection, and of the complex links between facts and interpretation,[9] but went in too much (like Livy) for the modernising of ancient times, while at the same time realising that people might think he was inventing early history. He carefully considered the writings of his predecessors, but the task of criticising them acutely was beyond him: he pursued form rather than content.

Linking rhetoric with political leadership and personal behaviour,[10] he looked favourably upon the political and analytic role of speeches,[11] and inserted (and invented) them when a classical model seemed to fit the situation.[12] In a separate work *On Thucydides* he had a lot to say about that writer's speeches, many of which, including the Melian Dialogue, he recognised to be inventions, even in substance.[13]

> Dionysius thought that Greek historical writing had begun in the form of histories of cities or regions based on local evidence – whether sacred or profane. . . . It is very doubtful, however, whether Dionysius knew of any history earlier than the fifth century BC.[14]

A number of writers in Latin, in addition to those who have been considered earlier in this book, also devoted themselves to this sort of field.

Cornelius Nepos

Cornelius Nepos (*c.* 99–24 BC), from Cisalpine Gaul, was a biographer rather than a historian (as were, later, Suetonius and Plutarch). But such was the current interest in personalities that the barrier between the two genres, if it had ever existed, had been cast down. He wrote a number of works on different subjects, and some of his biographies have disappeared, but many of the lives in his series *On Illustrious Men (De Viris Illustribus)* are still extant.

> Nepos was the writer of the first surviving biography in Latin. The idea of a parallel treatment of foreigners was probably taken from Marcus Terentius Varro's *Imagines*. His defects are hasty and careless composition (perhaps less marked in his first edition) and lack of control of his material.

He is mainly eulogistic, with an ethical aim, but also gives information about his hero's environment. As historian, his value is slight; he names many sources, but rarely used them at first hand. His style is essentially plain, but contains col-loquial features and many archaisms, not used for artistic effect, but from indifference. His rhetorical training appears in attempts at adornment, neither uniform nor discriminating.[15]

The biographies of Nepos hardly rank as serious works of research; indeed, he himself, echoing controversies on the subject, refused to claim that he was a historian.[16] He made a good many mistakes,[17] and included bogus miracles.[18] He was an apologist of Greekness. And he may have been deceived by propaganda directed against the Gracchi. However, he was right to deplore the fact that Cicero had not turned to history.[19]

Velleius Paterculus

Velleius Paterculus (c. 19 BC – after AD 30), of Campanian origin, wrote the *Historiae Romanae*, a brief account of Roman history addressed to a friend in order to celebrate the friend's consulship. It 'is enthusiastic rather than critical and has all the pretentiousness of the novice who has fallen under the spell of contemporary rhetoric'.[20]

The work is chiefly of interest today because Velleius so greatly admired Tiberius (under whom he had served), in contrast to Tacitus, to whom he therefore provides a counterpoise. He also believed in the phony *restituta respublica* of Augustus.[21] His evidence and interpretations, when he has not been an eye-witness, have to be used with care. He can, for example, plausibly forge a date.[22]

Quintus Curtius Rufus

Quintus Curtius Rufus may have written in the time of Claudius (AD 41–54). He wrote a history of Alexander the Great, of which three-quarters survives. He was rhetorical, vivid, romantic and emotional, and included fictitious speeches. He did not really claim to be a historian,[23] quite rightly, since he indulges in many sensational distortions and inconsistencies.[24] These include an account of the Persian landscape which is completely unauthentic, containing a reference to a river (the Medus) which did not exist.[25]

Three subsequent historians wrote in Greek.

Appian

Appian of Alexandria (born probably under Domitian, AD 81–96), wrote his *Romaica* under Antoninus Pius (AD 138–161). A large proportion of the work is extant. It treated Rome's conquests one after another, which was quite an old tradition. Although such a regional and ethnological scheme means a loss of continuity and chronology,[26] Appian has brought together some useful material, including a certain amount of economic information. But he is too devoted to Rome (where he had served as an advocate) and he is unreliable about Republican institutions and conditions.

Arrian

Arrian of Bithynia[27] governed Cappadocia under Hadrian (AD 117–138) and defeated the Alan invasion of 134. He was a student of the philosopher Epictetus, whose *Discourses* he preserved. His own chief book was the *Anabasis* (repeating the title of Xenophon's book), a story of Alexander the Great. But he also wrote the *Indike* and a *History* of Parthia (now lost). Arrian composed a plain and sober narrative, but, although realistic and shrewd, for example on matters of religion, he was unoriginal and had to rely too much upon a tradition that was favourable to Alexander.

Dio Cassius

Dio Cassius (Cassius Dio Cocceianus) of Nicaea was twice consul (*c.* AD 205, 229) and wrote not only a biography of Arrian and a study of the dreams and portents of Septimius Severus (193–211) but also a history of Rome from its beginnings to AD 229. A considerable part of the work is preserved, and other sections are represented in part or by epitomes. Dio misdates an Augustan conspiracy,[28] and is unreliable about Republican institutions and conditions, and his account of an alleged debate between Agrippa and Maecenas (the advisers of Augustus) is firmly anachronistic and 'modernised'.[29] He is also often wrong about Tiberius.[30]

Dio was aware that, even in earlier times, history had been hindered by fear or favour or friendship. He also knew very well that it was impossible to master the vast problems of the Roman empire,[31] of which the size and complexity put accurate knowledge out of reach. He wrote interestingly about the imperial secrecy which made accurate information even harder to obtain.[32]

> In later times most events began to be kept secret and were denied to common knowledge, and even though it may happen that some matters are made public, the reports are discredited because they cannot be investigated, and the suspicion grows that everything is said and done according to the wishes of the men in power at the time and their associates.
>
> In consequence much that never materialises becomes common talk, while much that has undoubtedly come to pass remains unknown. And in pretty well every instance the report which is spread abroad does not correspond with what actually happened.[33]

This meant that 'what could take place was talked of as having taken place, and what sounded at all plausible was taken as truth'.[34] Thus, Dio, somewhat discontentedly, had to be satisfied with the official version, because that was all he would get.[35]

He avoids precision and detail, since he does not want to inhibit his narrative flow. When details are included, they are sometimes fictitious.[36] His knowledge of Roman law is faulty,[37] and his chronology is not entirely consistent.[38]

Dio maintains a complete, unquestioned, identification with Rome, even at a time when there was quite a revival of Greek feeling.[39]

We return now to Latin writings.

Historia Augusta

The *Historia Augusta*,[40] compiled at a much later period to offer biographies of emperors and usurpers from AD 117 to 284, is quite absurdly fraudulent. It quotes documents that are manifestly spurious and contains at best, a few facts. This, perhaps, is done partly with tongue in cheek, with the intention of providing amusement, since Junius Tiberianus, prefect of the city, is quoted

105

(no doubt fictitiously) as taking a wholly sceptical view about history, which the writer of this work evidently accepts, or at least does not disagree with.

Eusebius

Eusebius of Caesarea Maritima in Syria Palaestina (*c.* AD 260–340) wrote a number of pieces in Greek, but his *Ecclesiastic History* was decisive. It was a model for all later ecclesiastical historians, but it overlooked many of the ablest pagan historians, since its emphasis throughout was on the triumph of the Church, a theme already made prominent by Melito of Sardes. Eusebius is important, however, because he quotes many documents.

Paulus Orosius

There was, of course, pagan opposition but this was countered by Orosius's *Historiae Adversus Paganos* (fifth century AD), showing that pagan disasters were even worse than those which had occurred under Christianity. But here we have moved far from history as it is generally understood.

Cassiodorus

Cassiodorus (*c.* AD 490–*c.* 583) is likewise confused, incoherent and inaccurate.[41]

LOST HISTORIANS

The works of a number of historians are lost or else survive only in fragments. If they were still extant, our picture of ancient historiography might be rather different. In addition, we should undoubtedly have a good deal more misinformation. One reason why these works have not survived is no doubt because, in many cases, they were not very well written.

First we may list a certain number of writings by Greeks, in the Greek language.

Hecataeus of Abdera

Hecataeus of Abdera, who flourished in *c.* 500 BC, was one of the earliest Ionian logographers (pioneers of history-writing). He wrote a *Periegesis*, a guide or journey round the world, of which more than three hundred fragments are extant (although the authenticity of many of them has been doubted.[1] He also illustrated a map. In addition, Hecataeus wrote a mythographic work, sometimes known as the *Genealogies* or *Heroology*.

He is famous for the remark: 'I write what I believe to be the truth, for the Greeks have many stories which, it seems to me, are absurd.'[2] This has been variously interpreted, as referring to epic tales or genealogies. Herodotus made use of Hecataeus, but was generally uncomplimentary about him.[3] Hecataeus's treatment of Persia stimulated new historical works.[4] But he was sneered at by Polybius for telling good stories.[5]

Hellanicus of Lesbos

Hellanicus of Lesbos was a contemporary of Herodotus whose writings have not come down to us, although fairly extensive fragments survive. He wrote mythographic works, and studies of regional history, and chronological surveys relating to local events. His accounts of foundations are unreliable, and his genealogies were full of inconsistencies: as Thucydides pointed out, his claim to chronological exactness is an illusion. His style was said to have been lacking in distinction.[6]

Ctesias of Cnidus

Ctesias of Cnidus flourished in the late fifth century BC. He wrote a history of Persia (in Ionic), a geographical treatise, and a pioneering separate work on India (*Indica*). He questioned the accuracy of Herodotus about Persian affairs, but was himself far from trustworthy, inventing documents and, in general, foreshadowing the romantic historical novel.[7]

Antiochus of Syracuse

Antiochus of Syracuse, in the fifth century BC, wrote a history of Sicily from mythical times to 424 BC (in the Ionic dialect), and a history of Italy (probably also in Ionic).

> He investigated the early history of Sicily and Italy and the plantation of the Greek colonies in those lands. . . . He was dealing with the subject of origins, in which the early historians inherited an interest from their epic predecessors, whose legends they supplemented and modified by local traditions. . . .
>
> But the great significance of Antiochus is that he wrote the modern and contemporary history of an important section of the Greek world. A comprehensive history of western Hellas was a step towards a comprehensive history of Hellas as a whole.[8]

Ephorus of Cyme

Ephorus of Cyme, *c.* 405–330 BC, wrote a Universal History (*Historiai*), telling of a succession of different hegemonies, as well as a history of Cyme, an essay on style, and a two-book work on various themes, such as readers of the period required (*Peri Heurematon*). We know him mainly through Diodorus Siculus (see p. 101), whose books 11–16 follow him closely. Polybius disliked him, because he slighted Arcadia, and so declared that he was weak on land warfare.[9] Ephorus was quite strong, however, on cultural history. But he admitted that archaic speeches (and deeds) could not be remembered,[10] although he himself made the speeches in his own works far too elaborate. He was too keen on panegyrics and 'probability',[11] and his Panhellenism prompted him to echo Isocrates on the superiority of the Greeks over the 'barbarians'. He went in a lot for moralising platitudes, but recognised that history and oratory, although closely allied, are not the same thing. History, in his view, was superior,[12] but he believed in moral edification by rhetoric and considered it a historian's duty to provide useful patterns of behaviour.[13]

Strabo, although he used Ephorus extensively, complained of his inaccuracies (like Polybius: see above) and disputed his claim to have excised the fabulous.[14] Ephorus was criticised for ignoring chronology, and his battle scenes, on which Polybius commented so unfavourably (n. 9 above), tended to be conventional.[15] Yet he was trusted because he did not go in too much for praise or blame,[16] and his influence was considerable.

> Ephorus's ambition was to produce, not antiquarian details, but a full account of past political and military events for the whole of Greece. A history of this scope had to define its own limits in relation to the mythical age, and was bound to involve an account of foreign nations (or 'barbarians') in their political conflicts and cultural contrasts with the Greeks. . . . [But] Ephorus was rather the founder of national history, and already displayed . . . patriotic prejudice. . . . In Ephorus universality existed only in the form of excursuses subordinated to Greek history.[17]

Theopompus of Chios

Theopompus of Chios (born *c.* 378 BC) wrote numerous historical works, including the *Hellenica* and *Philippica*, of which fragments survive. His aim was to display his rhetorical powers. He was famous for the severity of his verdicts, and willing to shock and exaggerate in order to force home moral lessons.[18] His second work, the life of Philip II of Macedonia, was full of enormous digressions.[19]

He was consciously offering world history, centred upon individuals, for educated general readers,[20] but Polybius attacked him for too much belief in miracles (which he condoned by stressing his talent for mythology)[21] – though Dionysius of Halicarnassus wrote favourably about his autopsy (see below).

Timaeus of Tauromenium

Timaeus of Tauromenium (*c.* 356–260 BC) wrote a huge history, primarily concerned with Sicily but also dealing with Italy, Libya and Greece. Polybius recognised his careful research and chronology (though based on clumsy, inconvenient Olympiads), but attacked him at enormous length,[22] for a variety of reasons (pp. 35, 48, 71, 96) and not least because of literary rivalry. Besides, Timaeus too greatly admired the Syracusan Timoleon, and hated Agathocles, the subsequent tyrant of the same city, who had been responsible for his banishment.[23]

Timaeus's failings as an historian largely resulted from his rhetorical training and were common to most of his contemporaries. He showed little critical ability in his fondness for rationalising myths and reliance on etymologies. But charges of wilful ignorance or falsification cannot be substantiated. And we must recognise in him the cultivation of wide interests characteristic of the Peripatetics [Aristotelians], diligence in collecting information, and a reasonable impartiality, except in the case of Agathocles.[24]

Aristotle

We know, from ancient accounts, of large collections of historical and scientific facts which were made by Aristotle (384–322 BC), sometimes in cooperation with others. The majority of these works have been lost, and exist only in fragments.[25]

A substantial part of his *Constitution of Athens* has survived on papyri (p. 121).

Callisthenes of Olynthus

Callisthenes of Olynthus, Aristotle's nephew, in the later fourth century wrote extravagantly in favour of Alexander III the Great, as champion of Panhellenism (against Greek opposition). But later he quarrelled with Alexander and was executed. Although he himself, it was said, had originally been an orator, he maintained that speeches must be appropriate to the speaker and the situation – in other words, their actual lack of authenticity did not matter. Vigorously criticised by Cicero, he indulged in rhetorical exaggeration and sensationalism.[26]

Duris of Samos

Duris of Samos (*c.* 340–260 BC), a pupil of Aristotle's successor Theophrastus, wrote various works on different subjects including *Histories* (370 – *c.* 280 BC), a *Samian Chronicle* and a *History of Agathocles* of Syracuse. Careless of style, but intensely interested in the theatre, he aimed at sensationalism and vivid emotional impact, dwelling on scandals and portents and eroticism. Cicero praised him.[27]

Clitarchus of Alexandria

Clitarchus of Alexandria (after 280) was another historian of Alexander, who was severely censured by ancient critics but became widely read in the early Roman empire. He portrayed the gorgeous east with fantasy.

Phylarchus of Athens

Phylarchus of Athens (third century BC) wrote a long history which drew largely on Duris but which entitled him to be regarded as the most important historian of his time. His moralising digressions are suspect, however, and he was deeply biased against Macedonia, which was partly why Polybius disliked him (pp. 42, 67), although he later also attacked him for appealing too much to the emotions.[28]

Posidonius

Posidonius of Apamea on the Orontes (c. 135 – c. 51–50 BC), after studying philosophy at Athens under the Stoic Panaetius, devoted several years of his life to scientific research in the western Mediterranean provinces and in north Africa. He then settled down at Rhodes, which became his adoptive country. Towards the end of 87 BC Posidonius was sent to Rome on behalf of the Rhodians to appease Marius, and he conceived for him an intense dislike.[29]

The meagreness of the fragments makes a reconstruction impossible. . . .[30]

In his *Histories*, which were biased in favour of the *nobilitas*,[31] and consequently strongly opposed to the Gracchi and the equestrian party, let alone the 'independent' Greeks, and their supporter Mithridates VI [of Pontus], Posidonius aimed at showing that the Roman empire, embracing as it did all the peoples of the world, embodied the commonwealth of mankind and reflected the commonwealth of God. . . .

Thus politics and ethics are one. . . . His travels and observations enabled him [to make scientific discoveries]. . . . He showed also a lively interest in poetry, rhetoric, lexicography, geometry, etc. . . . In the history of ancient thought he can be compared to no one but Aristotle.[32]

111

Posidonius attempted to reunite history with philosophy by showing that a universal 'sympathy' connected everything in the world.[33]

[He also] saw deeply into the social unrest of the period between 145 and c. 63 BC. He painted both the degeneration of the Hellenistic monarchies and the rapacity of the Roman capitalists.[34]

Posidonius continued the story of Roman history and expansion [after 146 BC]. As a historian, he seems to have laid particular emphasis on geographical and ethnographical considerations.

Probably less analytical than Polybius, Posidonius can be assumed to have written in a more colourful style.[35]

Alexander Polyhistor of Miletus

Alexander Polyhistor of Miletus, born c. 145 BC, came as a prisoner of war to Rome. Freed by Sulla, he took the name Lucius Cornelius Alexander. He was pedagogue to a Cornelius Lentulus, and later taught Gaius Julius Hyginus. He was accidentally burnt to death at Laurentum.

His vast literary output, probably after 49 BC, included compilations of material on various lands, Delphi, Rome, the Jews, wonder-stories, and literary criticism. . . .
Industrious and honest, he lacked taste and originality.[36]

One great savant, who was imported into Rome as a slave, Alexander Polyhistor (c. 70 BC), specialised in providing his masters with the ethnographical knowledge they needed to rule, or at least to enjoy the world they ruled.
One of his books, on the Jews, was sufficiently good to provide the Fathers of the Church with some of their most recondite quotations from Jewish writers.[37]

Now let us look at Roman historians, who wrote in Greek.

Quintus Fabius Pictor

The first name that we encounter in connection with lost Roman historians is that of Quintus Fabius Pictor. He took part in the

Second Punic War, and wrote a *History of Rome* in Greek, the earliest (so it was said) of a number of senatorial histories interpreting Rome to the Greek world – an unprecedented and presumptuous enterprise.

'Fabius's *History*', wrote A. H. McDonald, 'probably owed more to Hellenistic historiography than to the pontifical tradition.'[38] But it was a chauvinistic work (the model for others), which could not be swallowed whole, and was criticised by Polybius – despite Fabius's senatorial status.[39] Of this Fabius was proudly conscious, and he glorified his family.[40] He was eager to explain the moral qualities of the Romans to the Greeks, and thus to further Roman policy in the Greek world. In this he has been described as scarcely successful.[41]

Aulus Postumius Albinus

Aulus Postumius Albinus (consul 151 BC) was an enthusiastic phil-Hellene who wrote his *History of Rome* in Greek, although Cato the elder mocked his use of the language.[42] Polybius recognised his culture and influence, but grudgingly and critically, because Albinus refused to allow the Achaean exiles to return home.

Next we come to the Romans who wrote in Latin.

Marcus Porcius Cato 'Censorius'

Marcus Porcius Cato 'Censorius' of Tusculum (234–149 BC; Cato the elder) published numerous speeches and wrote historical books, including the lost *Origines* (c. 168–149), perhaps the first work of its kind in Latin, on which Roman prose style was based. Though by no means an enemy of the established order, he waged steady warfare against birth and class. His attitude to the Greeks was ambivalent. His speeches varied from accurate reporting to autobiographical polemic.[43] He employed simple rhetorical devices.

Cnaeus Gellius

Cnaeus Gellius (second century BC) wrote a *History of Rome* from its origins to at least 146 BC. His work was full, probably because he was able to use the *Annales Maximi*, now published.[44] He elaborated his source material by the (apparently not very skilful) employment of rhetorical methods, and went in for a good deal of invention, based on 'probability' (pp. 43–4).[45] His main purpose was to entertain.

Gaius Fannius

Gaius Fannius (consul 122 BC) wrote a *History*, perhaps concentrating on his own time, in which he included verbatim reports of speeches and described contemporary personalities. He was concerned to defend his own record and, particularly, his move from one political side to the other.[46]

Sempronius Asellio

Sempronius Asellio (military tribune 134–133 BC) wrote a history of his times in his own 'pragmatic' (i.e. more scientific) style which, in a surviving fragment, he distinguished from the usual annalistic (year by year) form (see *Annales Maximi*, p. 158). His main purpose was patriotic, since he maintained that histories should make their readers readier to defend their state.[47]

Lucius Coelius Antipater

Lucius Coelius Antipater (writing after 121 BC) introduced the historical monograph to Rome, composing, after Hellenistic models, a long work on the Second Punic War. He went in for artistic presentation; for arresting, vivid rhythm and word-order, employing his rhetorical training to achieve political effects, and inventing speeches to improve the picture. Cicero laughed at him but praised him, and Livy made use of his work.[48]

Marcus Aemilius Scaurus

Marcus Aemilius Scaurus (consul in 115 BC) was a powerful leader of the senate who wrote an autobiography (*De Vita Sua*) to defend his own record.[49]

Publius Rutilius Rufus

Publius Rutilius Rufus (consul in 105 BC) wrote a history of his own time, full of acid, embittered allusions to people with whom he disagreed.[50]

Valerius Antias

Valerius Antias (early first century BC, of Antium) wrote a *History of Rome*. It was fuller than the evidence justified (although Antias knew something about the documents which he apparently quoted), and contained fictitious battle scenes and casualty figures and speeches, distorted by political and family influences[51] and by patriotic urges, such as the invention of 'treaties broken by Carthage'.[52] He admired Sulla, whose enemy Marius had been unkind to his home-town of Antium. Livy deplored the exaggerations of Antias,[53] but made use of him, with caution.[54]

Quintus Claudius Quadrigarius

Quintus Claudius Quadrigarius, another post-Sullan annalist, likewise wrote an extensive *History of Rome*. Surviving fragments show that his style was fairly simple. He invented documents, and allowed poignant anecdotes to run riot. His aim was to entertain his readers.[55]

Lucius Cornelius Sisenna

Lucius Cornelius Sisenna (praetor 78 BC) wrote *Histories* which, after a reference to Roman origins, treated the Social (Marsic, Italic) War (91–87 BC) and Sullan Civil War. He was strongly in favour of Sulla, and offered vigorous views. Sallust pronounced him to be 'disingenuous'. His composition was literary rather than chronological, and his style vivid and arresting.[56]

Gaius Licinius Macer

Gaius Licinius Macer (consul 66 BC) was yet another writer of a *History of Rome*. It was full of rationalised legends, and made use of the *libri lintei* ('Linen Books') which were not nearly as old as was supposed. Macer was a Marian, committed to bitter antagonism to Sulla, and showed the usual favour to his own family. A good deal of what he wrote was reproduced by Livy.[57]

Marcus Terentius Varro

Marcus Terentius Varro (116–27 BC), probably from Reate, was the most learned man of the age. His numerous works included a social *History of the Roman People* (*De Vita Populi Romani*), and the *De Gente Populi Romani* on archaic Rome and its chronological problems. The character sketches in these historical writings were apparently interesting, as, indeed, they are in his surviving compilations, such as his *Antiquities* (*Antiquitates Rerum Humanarum ac Divinarum*). He was prepared to admit Greeks among his ancestral portraits.[58]

Gaius Asinius Pollio

Gaius Asinius Pollio (76 BC – AD 4), consul in 40 BC, built the first public library in Rome, and retired from politics to devote himself to literature, and above all to history. His *Historiae* covered the period from 60 to 42 BC.

He criticised Cicero and Caesar, disliked Sallust's archaism, and found provincial *Patavinitas* in Livy. Writing somewhat carelessly, without a strict regard for the truth but, instead, with a considerable measure of truculence, he gave an inaccurate account of his own doings, either on purpose or possibly (in part) through forgetfulness. As to history in general, however, he detested efforts to make it improving and he condemned the idea that it should be moral or romantic.[59]

Tiberianus asserted that much of Pollio's work besides being too brief, was too careless.

> But when I said, in reply, that there was no writer, at least in the realm of history, who had not made some false statement, and even pointed out the places in which Livy and Sallust, Cornelius Tacitus, and, finally, Trogus could be refuted by manifest proofs, he came over wholly to my opinion, and, throwing up his hands, he jestingly said besides: 'Well, then, write as you will. You will be safe in saying whatever you wish, since you will have as comrades

in falsehood those authors whom we admire for the style of their histories.'[60]

The Christian writers are quite obvious falsifiers of history in the interests of their world picture.[61]

Trogus

Trogus was a Vocontian from Narbonese Gaul, in the time of Augustus (35 BC – AD 14). His work is preserved only in an epitome. In addition to other compositions, he wrote a massive Universal History, the *Historiae Philippicae*, which was elaborated, in Hellenistic fashion, by dramatic techniques and a powerful moralising element. The work is undistinguished, derivative and confused.

Trogus attacked the speeches of Livy as fakes, and did not include any himself.[62]

Sextus Julius Africanus

Sextus Julius Africanus was a Christian historian and philosopher from Jerusalem (Aelia Capitolina), who wrote in Greek not only a miscellany (*kestoi*) but also Chronographies up to AD 221 which are full of mathematical symbolism and fantasy.

In his time Africanus was a figure of considerable interest. . . . He travelled widely. . . . In *c.* AD 220 he settled at Emmaus (renamed Nicopolis) in Palestine, whence in 222 he travelled to Rome on an embassy for his city. At Rome he so impressed the emperor Severus Alexander (222–235) by his erudition that the emperor entrusted him with the building of his library at the Pantheon in Rome.

His learning was that of a typical antiquarian. He compiled a chronicle of world history, placing the Incarnation in the 5500th year after the creation. He also wrote a voluminous miscellany, similar in content to the elder Pliny's *Natural History*. . . .

Africanus was the first Christian whose writings were not all concerned with the faith. Africanus's attitude to the Bible was likewise antiquarian in character. He harmonised the Gospel genealogies, and noticed that the History of Susanna contains an atrocious Greek pun.[63]

The pagan Porphyry endeavoured to refute Africanus's claim that Biblical monotheism was the oldest of all religions.[64]

INFORMATION FROM OTHER SOURCES

Literary Works

Much may also be learned from literary works besides the historical: epic and other poetry, tragic or comic plays, speeches, philosophical treatises, novels. Many of these works are, like histories, the product of a restricted social class and so share its limited vision, but they may also be unconsciously revealing with regard to its assumptions and preconceptions. These literary products of the Greco-Roman world are in varying degrees alien to us and pose considerable problems of interpretation.[1]

> It is a great mistake to suppose that historical experience is expressed in so-called historical records alone.... Greek historical experience or mental history is better expressed in Greek literature than ours is in the literature of modern Europe.... The surviving masterpieces of Greek literature give a better insight into the subjective side of Greek history... than any insight into the subjective side of modern history which we can obtain by studying it through modern literature.[2]

Since historiography depended a great deal upon the epic, and upon tragic poetry as well (pp. 25–30), it is not surprising that both of these genres provide a good deal of material that contributes to our knowledge of what was happening. As regards other forms of Greek literature, it is probably the Old Comedy of Aristophanes which is most valuable to the historian.

> The use for historical purposes of the so-called Old Comedy may be of various kinds. In the first place, there is the general political significance of comedy itself in the Athenian social and cultural context.
>
> Meanings are much more wide-ranging and explicit than is the case with tragedy. For the people as a whole played its part by sharing the views of the author, in the sense that the author, by free and open discussion of political themes,

sought deliberately to be an exponent and interpreter of widely-held opinions. . . .

If a modern historian can grasp the reflection of reality in Attic comedy, he will be able to reconstruct the actuality of Athenian society and economy.[3]

But that is just one of the innumerable branches of Greek and Latin literature which has something to tell us about the historical process. The novel is, of course, another, very conspicuous example.

Archaeology

The modern historian, trying to find out something about the Greek and Roman world, is also enormously dependent on non-literary sources, among which archaeology is especially useful.

The experience [of classical archaeology] has revealed certain assets on the part of archaeological evidence in a historical context. . . . Excavated physical remains, at least at the moment of their discovery, do bring us closer to some kind of historical reality than we are ever likely to get through any other medium.[4]

In classical archaeology – the study of the material remains of the Greeks and Etruscans and Romans – the last few decades have in many countries produced new discoveries of many kinds, and of many ancient epochs, telling us a great deal about the things that happened, and why they happened as they did. These discoveries have enlarged, and indeed transformed, our knowledge of classical history. . . . The classical historian has an absolute need of the archaeologist: archaeology is visible history. . . . There are, in fact, immense and varied contributions to our still very defective knowledge of ancient history that classical archaeology has yet to make. Indeed, it is busy doing so at this very moment – stimulated by enlarged public interest – on an even more breathtaking scale than the past three decades have witnessed.[5]

There is no need to list here the countless archaeological sites which throw essential light on the history of the Greek and Roman world. They have provided invaluable information, for instance, about architecture, and about art of many kinds.

Inscriptions have served a similar purpose.

> If the making and display of inscriptions is attested in many cultures, it was so distinctive a feature of Greco-Roman civilisation that it deserves consideration as a major cultural phenomenon in its own right.
>
> As a consequence of this, the sheer volume of inscriptions from the ancient world, primarily but not only in Greek and Latin, gives epigraphy a central importance in the study of its history and culture. . . . Inscriptions, read in bulk, provide the most direct access which we can have to the life, social structure, thought and values of the ancient world.[6]

Papyrology

Another branch of archaeology, if it should be so defined, which has been especially useful to the historian is papyrology.

> Papyri and parchments, which may preserve public documents but also offer us thousands of examples of private, informal texts – letters, complaints, records of dreams, private financial accounts – are potentially even more revealing [than inscriptions].
>
> But the very special circumstances required for their preservation, which are consistently present only in the desert areas of Middle and Upper Egypt and in parts of the Near East, inevitably create a marked geographical bias in the evidence which they present.[7] Apart from the charred remains of a library in Herculaneum, it is the dry sands of Egypt covering classical sites which have furnished such material. After several chance discoveries in the latter half of the nineteenth century, the nineties witnessed systematic excavations which greatly advanced classical learning in all fields. Oxyrhynchus [is particularly rich] in literary texts.[8]

The particular relevance of papyrology to the present book lies in the fact that Oxyrhynchus has contributed an important historical writer, known as the Oxyrhynchus Historian.

> In 1906 some 900 lines of a lost Greek historian were discovered at Oxyrhynchus in Egypt. The writer dealt in con-

siderable detail with events in the Greek world, 396–395 BC, and was an authority of the first importance. The papyrus indicates a strict chronological arrangement by summers and winters, competent criticism and analysis of motives, a first hand knowledge of the topography of Asia Minor, and certain details found in no other work of the period.

It was probably a continuation of Thucydides beginning with the autumn of 411, was written between 387 and 346, and its elaborate scale suggests that it covered only a short period. . . . Three further fragments (90 lines) were published in 1949.[9]

The publication in 1907 of the celebrated fragment from the writer who must still be called the Oxyrhynchus historian has promoted one of the most entertaining controversies of the literary history of antiquity, and one which suggests some chastening reflections. . . . Three shorter fragments of the same work (amounting to some ninety lines in all) published in 1940 do not assist towards the solution [of authorship], though they give some useful confirmation on other points . . .

But what sort of historian? A more than respectable one, it would appear. In style, dull but unobjectionable; in chronological exactness superior to Xenophon. . . .

If such a historian as this is in fact one who is not even known to us by name, this is a sobering thought. . . .

But the importance of *Hellenica Oxyrhynchia* in these years since its rediscovery goes beyond this question of authorship, and beyond the new information it has yielded. It lies most of all in the stimulus it has given to the study of the fourth-century historians in general, and to the lessons which it has taught us here. It has taught us to know (among other things) our own limitations.[10]

The papyri have also provided a second significant historical work.

That other great gift of the papyri, *The Constitution of Athens* (*Athenaion Politeia*) has continued to inspire fruitful studies even after the intense activity of its first twenty years subsided.

Here the question of authorship may be considered as of secondary importance, since it has never been in doubt that this is the work which antiquity itself recognised as Aristotle's *Constitution*.

What has been called more in question . . . is the reliance to be placed on the work by us. . . . [But] undoubtedly the most important historiographical result of the appearance of *Athenaion Politeia* was the stimulus which it provided to the study of its own sources, which prove to be certain of the writers of Athenian history (*Atthides*) of the generation immediately before Aristotle's own.[11]

Coinage

Coinage too has a great deal to offer to the historian. Hundreds of Greek and Greco-Roman cities coined; and from their coins we learn far more about them than the ancient historians bothered to tell us. Also, the members of eminent Roman families reveal much of their histories on Roman Republican coins. Later on, Roman emperors issued an astonishingly large and varied series of coin-types which throw enormous light on what was going on or on what the emperors wished people to think was going on.

Numismatics is not an autonomous subject – it is part of history, and work on coinage is best done by people who are primarily historians or archaeologists, who use coinage to help to solve the problems which relate to their interests, whether in financial administration, the fiscal needs of a state, unity of reckoning, monetary usages, interpretation of types, art history, or the dating of archaeological levels.[12]

The imperial coinage of Rome remains one of the major testimonies of the power of the Roman government in its heyday, and to the strength of the ideal Rome in its decline.[13]

Because of all of these other sources of information, besides the Greek and Roman historians themselves, we need not be entirely sceptical – as many are[14] – about the possibility of learning about the ancient world.

MISINFORMATION FROM OTHER SOURCES

Archaeology

We have seen how the greater historians lavish misinformation upon us. The lesser historians do so too, whether their works are still extant or lost (pp. 100–18), and likewise other Greek and Roman writers.

We must not think that archaeology, which gives us so much valuable information, is immune from the charge of giving us misinformation as well. For example, the Temple of Castor and Pollux in the Forum at Rome was erected to honour an occasion which was entirely fictitious.

> It was said that the Latins supported the ejected tyrant Tarquinius Superbus and fought against the Romans in 499 or 496 BC at Lake Regillus, fourteen miles away from the city.... Before news of the battle had reached Rome, two young warriors were seen in the Forum, watering their white horses at the Spring of Juturna beside the site where this temple was later founded.... Before vanishing from the eyes of men, the horsemen announced a great victory. And in this they themselves had played the leading part.
>
> The Romans understood who their visitors had been, and built this temple for their worship, dedicating it in 484 BC.[1]

The temple was built to commemorate an epiphany which was miraculous and which, in fact, never happened.

The alleged Christian discoveries by Constantine's mother Helena in the Holy Land show unmercifully how such archaeological data could be forged.

> With the assistance of the natives, who no doubt did not go unrewarded, she had located, to her own satisfaction, all the spots where every important event in the recorded career of Jesus at Jerusalem took place. She had arranged for each of these places to be dug up, and promptly identified what was found there to her own satisfaction.
>
> The authenticity of these finds, dating back, as was alleged, to a so much earlier time – the tomb, Golgotha, the True Cross, and the locations where Jesus was born and ascended to heaven – has aroused scepticism, which is hardly surprising. A scholar has commented that her thrilling discoveries

were made 'with miraculous aid seldom now vouchsafed to archaeologists'.[2]

Ancient Art

Ancient art sometimes plays a similar part in the embellishment or falsification of history. It is especially visible in the portrait-busts of eminent Greeks and Romans. Often they idealise their subjects to such an extent that the busts bear little or no relation to what the men or women really looked like. A good example is provided by the statue of the Roman emperor Claudius in the Vatican Museum. He is made to resemble Jupiter, which makes a mockery of his real, undistinguished appearance.[3]

Inscriptions

Inscriptions can be equally deceptive. An example is provided by Troezen in the Peloponnese.

> In 480 BC Troezen had welcomed and supported Athenian refugees. Some two hundred years after the event she set up this 'copy' of the decree of Themistocles to recall her links with Athens in the great days, presumably to confirm or improve current relations. . . . No one can now believe that this is an accurate copy of a decree passed in 480. . . . It is difficult to believe that a true copy can have survived.[4]

And, many centuries later, much in Augustus's *Res Gestae* (*Monumentum Ancyranum*) – notably the reference to the 'restoration of the *respublica*' – is manifestly imperial propaganda.[5]

Coins

The inscriptions on coins are, on occasion, equally fraudulent. Roman Republican moneyers showed completely fictitious pictures of their alleged ancestors on their coins (cf. also portrait-busts).[6] Another blatant instance – unless we prefer to think of it as expressing an optimistic hope – is the PAX ORBIS TER-RARVM (Peace Throughout the World) of Otho (AD 69),[7] at a time when the Roman empire was racked by civil war.

Coins also (like later writers) record that Septimius Severus (AD

193–211) declared himself the son of Marcus Aurelius,[8] which he was not.

> Soon after his first victory, Septimius took a remarkable step. He proclaimed himself to be the son of Marcus Aurelius. In the first bronze issue which gives him the titles that celebrate his victories, one *sestertius* describes him as 'Son of the deified Marcus Pius'.[9]

There are also ambiguous cases. When Hadrian in AD 117 declared on a coin that he was the adopted son of the recently deceased Trajan,[10] it is uncertain whether his claim was truthful or untruthful: probably the latter, but no one can now be sure.

> Scepticism, if secret, was none the less rife. As was bound to happen under the circumstances, rumours of all kinds were current.... [Many] regarded the letters of adoption as a forgery.... We do not know why Trajan was so late in adopting a successor nor whether the death-bed adoption [at Selinus] is true.[11]

At first Trajan's wife Plotina said nothing about her husband's death; then she dispatched a letter to the senate announcing the death-bed adoption of Hadrian. The senate, however doubtful, accepted the message, because Hadrian had the support of the eastern armies.

Papyri

The papyri, too, not only inform us but also misinform us. The Aristotelian *Constitution of Athens* (*Athenaion Politeia*) is a prime example. Despite its great value to historians (pp. 110, 121), it is misleading. For one thing, its 'loyal and respectful treatment of the development of Athens' is by no means objective.[12] But there is more to it than that. The historical part of the *Constitution* shows an 'unskilful blending of discrepant traditions'.[13] Moreover, 'there is some disappointment over many mistakes and a certain aristocratic prejudice, as, for instance, in the criticism of the coup of 411 BC. It is apparent that Aristotle worked in a hurry and was dependent on sources which were not always reliable.'[14]

CONCLUSION

At the beginning, I offered a warning that one must expect a good deal of inadequacy and misinformation from the ancient historians, but that there were several excellent reasons for studying them all the same. The intention of this book has been to argue, despite all of the hazards and problems, that we ought to be cautious, but at the same time not too pessimistic, about the reconstruction of the Greek and Roman past.

True, there are certain grounds for pessimism, and we do not have to go back to the ancient past to find them. In looking at the events of our own time, we are surrounded by misinformation on every side. Who can claim that he or she has the slightest idea of what is really happening today? Name any country that is undergoing a crisis, anywhere. Are we really able to suppose that we can understand what is happening there? Of course not. There are many conflicting accounts, and some or all of them are untrue. The same applies even to our own country. Can we trust anyone to tell us, reliably, what is going on? We cannot.

If that is the case with events today, how much more so is it the case with events that happened many centuries ago! Pity the poor historians. How desperately difficult it is for them to find out and describe, accurately, what took place at some date in the past. The proof of this lies in the extraordinarily varied and contradictory versions that emerge. These have prompted post-modernists and others to deny that any reliable historical record can be reconstructed at all.[1] But that is unduly defeatist. It can be reconstructed, to a considerable extent, and that applies to the Greek and Roman as well as to subsequent civilisations. However, this can be done only if we look at their own historians firmly and frankly and unflinchingly; if we note, despite the literary excellence of many of them, what are their faults or at least their differences from what we require, or ought to require, today. That is what this book has tried to do, with regard to the Greco-Roman world.

ABBREVIATIONS

AC	A. Cameron (ed.) *History as Text*, 1989
AM	A. Momigliano, *Studies in Historiography*, 1966
CWF	C. W. Fornara, *The Nature of History in Ancient Greece and Rome*, 1983
FJT	F. J. Teggart, *Theory and Processes of History*, 1972
FMC	F. M. Cornford, *Thucydides Mythistoricus*, 1907, 1965
FWW	F. W. Walbank, *Polybius*, 1972, 1990
GHLH	*The Greek Historians; Literature and History* (papers presented to A. E. Raubitschek), 1985
HEB	H. E. Barnes, *A History of Historical Writing*, 1937, 1962
HHA	*Histoire et Historiens dans l'Antiquité* (Fondation Hardt, Entretiens sur l'Antiquité Classique, iv), 1956
JBB	J. B. Bury, *Ancient Greek Historians*, 1908, 1958
JP	J. Percival, *Truth in the Greek and Roman Historians* (lecture), 1991
JRS	*Journal of Roman Studies*
MC	M. Crawford (ed.) *Sources for Ancient History*, 1983
MG/*AH*	M. Grant, *The Ancient Historians*, 1970
MG/*RCH*	M. Grant, *Readings in the Classical Historians*, 1992.
MIF/*AH*	M. I. Finley, *Ancient History*, 1985
MIF/*UAH*	M. I. Finley, *The Use and Abuse of History*, 1971
MIF/*LGNA*	M. I. Finley (ed.) *The Legacy of Greece: A New Appraisal*, 1981
MP	M. Platnauer (ed.) *Fifty Years (and Twelve) of Classical Scholarship*, 1968
OCD	*Oxford Classical Dictionary* (2nd edn, 1970)
PGW	P. G. Walsh, *Livy: His Historical Aims and Methods*, 1967
PP	P. Plass, *Wit and the Writing of History: The Rhetoric*

	of Historiography in Imperial Rome, 1988
RMa	R. Martin, *Tacitus*, 1981
RMe	R. Mellor, *Tacitus*, 1993
RS/*FH*	R. Syme, *Fictional History Old and New: Hadrian* (Lecture), 1984
RS/*S*	R. Syme, *Sallust*, 1964
RS/*T*	R. Syme, *Tacitus*, 1958
RS/*TST*	R. Syme, *Ten Studies in Tacitus*, 1970
SU	S. Usher, *The Historians of Greece and Rome*, 1969
TAD/*L*	T. A. Dorey (ed.) *Livy*, 1971
TAD/*LB*	T. A. Dorey (ed.) *Latin Biography*, 1967
TAD/*LH*	T. A. Dorey (ed.) *Latin Historians*, 1966
TAD/*T*	T. A. Dorey (ed.) *Tacitus*, 1969

NOTES

INTRODUCTION

1 M. Grant, *A Short History of Classical Civilization* (1991), p. 1; cf. *Gallatin Review* XII. 1, 1992/3, pp. 57ff.
2 MG/*AH*.
3 P. J. Rhodes has written in defence of the Greek historians, *Greece and Rome* 2nd ser. XII. 2, 1994, pp. 156–71.
4 The question whether biographers were historians has long been discussed. Cf. A. Momigliano, *The Development of Greek Biography* (1971).

1 ANCIENT AND MODERN HISTORIANS

The Historians of Greece and Rome

1 E. Gabba, in MC, pp. 3f, 24.
2 Ibid, p. 4.
3 Herodotus improved on earlier writings, MG/*AH*, pp. 65f.
4 R. W. Macan, *Cambridge Ancient History* V (1935), p. 417.
5 Yet there was no word for 'history' until Herodotus invented it: W. G. Forrest, *Herodotus*, p. xxxiv; and it could be said that before the fifth century BC no Greek historical writing existed, MIF/*UAH*, p. 216 no. 19.
6 History, to Herodotus, also meant ethnography and archaeology; and he was the source of many literary forms.
7 Cicero, *On Laws*, I.1.5. Cf. also AM, p. 127.
8 JBB, p. 81.
9 MG/*RCH*, p. 62.
10 I.22, MG/*AH*, p. 81.
11 JBB, pp. 109f., RS/*S*, p. 260; 'awkward weightiness', P. Levi, *A History of Greek Literature*, 1985; p. 289.
12 JBB, p. 147.
13 H. T. Wade-Gery, *OCD*, p. 1069.
14 AM, p. 218.

15 F. W. Walbank, in TAD/*LH*, p. 59 etc. Verbose, laborious, unfresh, unnatural, unsmooth, monotonous. But defended as simple and direct.
16 JBB, pp. 218, 212.
17 E. Gabba, in MC, p. 13.
18 A. Momigliano, in MIF/*LGNA*, pp. 172f.
19 G. T. Griffith, in MP, p. 201; cf. p. 203.
20 F. W. Walbank, in TAD/*LH*, p . 19.
21 MG/*RCH*, pp. 189f. It is very doubtful if he only intended to provide source material, T. A. Dorey, in TAD/*LH*, p. 84; cf. p. 66.
22 Did his public career end after his governorship of Africa Nova, or after Caesar's death? G. M. Paul, in TAD/*LH*, p. 94.
23 *Sera et severa oratio*, Gellius, 17, 18. Cf. RS/*S*, pp. 261, 263, 296.
24 RS/*S*, p. 272.
25 MG/*AH*, p. 211.
26 MG/*RCH*, p. 266.
27 RS/*S*, p. 272, cf. pp. 297, 301.
28 C. T. Cruttwell, *A History of Roman Literature* (6th edn, 1898), p. 200.
29 G. M. Paul, in TAD/*LH*, pp. 96, 105, 107 no. 98, 112 n. 86.
30 RMe, p. 172 no. 11, suggests that Livy's talents were probably best displayed in his lost books.
31 Wrongly, according to P. G. Walsh, in TAD/*LH*, p. 137.
32 T. A. Dorey, in TAD/*L*, p. xi.
33 Quintilian x.1, 32.
34 P. G. Walsh, *Livy*, pp. 173, 177.
35 C. T. Cruttwell, *A History of Roman Literature*, 6th edn (1898), p. 326.
36 A. Lesky, *A History of Greek Literature* (2nd edn, 1966), p. 805.
37 Jerome, *Letters*, 22.35; cf. M. Hadas-Lebel, *Flavius Josephus* (1993), p. 2.
38 MG/*RCH*, p. 405.
39 D. A. Russell, *Plutarch* (1973), p. 21.
40 MG/*RCH*, p. 458.
41 N. P. Miller, in TAD/*T*, pp. 106f, 112.
42 Tacitus, *Annals*, IV.33.
43 Cf. M. L. W. Laistner, *The Greater Roman Historians* (1947), p. 123, *pace* N. P. Miller, in TAD/*T*, p. 99.
44 *Scriptores Historiae Augustae, Probus*, 2.7.
45 E. A. Thompson, in TAD/*LH*, p. 155.
46 R. Syme, *Ammianus and the Historia Augusta* (1968), pp. 94f.
47 E. Gibbon, *Decline and Fall of the Roman Empire* (1776–88), Ch. XXXI.

2 THE HISTORIANS AND OTHER DISCIPLINES

History and Poetry

1 FWW, p. 1: fact and myth were not clearly differentiated, MIF/*UAH*, pp. 15ff. On history and poetry, cf. A. Cameron in AC, p. 10.
2 Which it was not: M. I. Finlay, *Aspects of Antiquity* (1968), pp. 28ff.

Cf. P. Wathelet, *Les Troyens de l'Iliade: mythe et histoire* (1989). But the ancients *felt* the epic past, cf. H. Meyerhoff, *Time in Literature*, p. 33, MIF/*UAH*, p. 33.

3 There was, eventually, an 'affirmation of discontinuity between myth and history', S. G. Pembroke, in MIF/*LGNA*, p. 303.

4 JBB, p. 17.

5 Juvenal, 15.13–16: cf. C. H. Taylor (ed.) *Essays on the Odyssey* (1965), p. 67; cf. E. Bowie in C. Gill and T. P. Wiseman (eds) *Lies and Fiction in the Ancient World* (1993), p. 19; cf. T. P. Wiseman, ibid, p. 137.

6 Cf. J. V. Morrison, *Homeric Misdirection: False Predictions in the Iliad* (1992).

7 For Xenophanes, JBB, p. 10 no. 1, and for Eratosthenes Strabo VII, 3.6; cf. 1.23–25.

8 Hesiod, *Theogony*, 27–28. JBB, p. 5 nn. 1, 7, suggests that Hesiod's *Theogony* contains the first crude idea of the history of civilisation.

9 Plato, *Republic*, II, 377d. 4–6.

10 As Theagenes of Rhegium did, JBB, p. 10 n. 1. Archilochus's 'quarrel with the family of Lycambes' (fr. 24, Horace, *Epistles*, I. 19. 23ff) might be fictitious: cf. discussion by P. E. Easterling and B. M. W. Knox, *Cambridge History of Classical Literature*, I. *Greek Literature* (1985), pp. 118f.

11 Hecataeus, fragment 1.

12 CWF, pp. 3f, 12.

13 Herodotus, 1.5, 3.122.

14 Herodotus's relative and fellow-townsman Panyassis sought to 'resuscitate' the epic.

15 J. T. Shotwell, *An Introduction to the History of History* (1922), HEB, p. 29.

16 Aristotle, *Generation of Animals*, 3.5.16; *logopoios* according to Arrian, *Anabasis*, III.30 (Herodotus used the same word about Hecataeus, II.143, v.36, 125). It has been said that Herodotus invented the conversion of legend-writing into the science of history, R. G. Collingwood, *The Idea of History* (1946), p. 19.

17 JBB, p. 81, HEB, p. 30.

18 Herodotus, 1.9, 10.1, 10.3–5, 11.1–2.

19 SU, p. 36.

20 Polybius, XXXIV; cf. F. W. Walbank, in TAD/*LH*, p. 54 and nn. 118–120.

21 Cf. Livy's preface to Book I.

22 Livy, II, 20.1ff; cf. Homer, *Iliad*, III, 15ff.

23 Livy, II, 19ff; cf. J. Briscoe, in TAD/*L*, p. 13.

24 Livy, XXII, 47ff; cf. SU, p. 171.

25 RMe, p. 21.

26 F. Leo, *Tacitus* (1896); V. Pöschl (ed.) *Tacitus* (1969).

27 Cf. A. J. Gossage, in TAD/*LB*, p. 64.

28 A. Momigliano, in MIF/*LGNA*, p. 156.

29 M. I. Finley, *History and Theory*, IV, 1965, p. 282.

30 Aristotle, *Poetics*, IX, 1451 B.5–7 (tr. I. Bywater); cf. G. E. M. de Sainte Croix, 'Aristotle on History and Poetry', in B. Levick (ed.) *The Ancient Historian and His Materials* (1975), pp. 45–88, K. von Fritz,

Die Bedeutung des Aristoteles für die Geschichtsschreibung, M. J. Wheeldon, in AC, p. 61, MIF/*UAH*, p. 11.

31 E. Gabba, in MC, pp. 51, 53; cf. F. W. Walbank, 'History and Tragedy', *Historia* IX, 1960, pp. 216ff.

32 *Papyri from Oxyrhynchus*, 23 (1956), no. 2382, MG/*AH*, p. 51.

33 G. T. Griffith, in MP, p. 190; cf. C. MacLeod, *Collected Essays* (1983), pp. 140–58. For Thucydides's strong sense of drama, cf. A. Cameron, in AC, p. 208.

34 Cf. PGW, p. 25.

35 Polybius, II, 5.6.11 (tr. R. Paton).

36 Cf. F. W. Walbank, *Bulletin of the Institute of Classical Studies*, II, 1955, p. 4, *Selected Papers* (1985), pp. 212f, JBB, pp. 172f, R. Ullmann, *Transactions of the American Philological Association*, XXIII, 1942, p. 43.

37 Cicero, *Laws*, I, 1.5.

38 Cicero, *Letters to Friends*, V, 12.6.

39 T. A. Dorey, in TAD/*LH*, p. 75.

40 R. Ullmann, *Revue philologique*, LXII, 1918, pp. 3ff.

41 PGW, p. 196.

42 Quintilian X, 1, 31.

43 Plutarch, *On the Glory of the Athenians* (*Moralia* 347).

44 Plutarch, *On the Malice of Herodotus*, 3,855D. And he regarded poetry as deceitful, *Moralia* 16.

45 E. Segal, 'Tacitus and Poetic History', *Ramus* II, 1978, pp. 107–26.

46 SU, p. 220.

47 Cf. A. Wallace-Hadrill, in W. Hamilton and A. Wallace-Hadrill, *Ammianus Marcellinus: The Later Roman Empire* (AD 354–378) (1986), p. 27.

48 Though H. J. Muller, *The Uses of the Past* (1952), p. 42, regards our interest in history as 'more poetic than practical or scientific'.

History and Rhetoric and Philosophy

1 H. White, in H. White and P. E. Manuel (eds) *Theories of History* (1978), M. J. Wheeldon, in AC, p. 53 (quoting T. Jansen, *Latin Prose Prefaces*, 1964).

2 A. J. Woodman, *Rhetoric in Classical Historiography: Four Studies* (1988), reviewed by R. Brock, *Liverpool Classical Monthly* 16/7/91, pp. 97–102, J. C. Moles, *History of the Human Sciences*, XXXII, 1990, pp. 317–21, I. Worthington (ed.) *Persuasion: Greek Rhetoric in Action* (1994), T. M. Conley, *Rhetoric in the European Tradition* (1994), A. Cameron, in AC, p. 10.

3 For the heritage of Isocrates see MIF/*UAH*, pp. 193–214; cf. in general A. Momigliano in E. S. Shaffer (ed.) *Comparative Criticism*, III, 1981, pp. 254–68, and in *Daily Telegraph* 22/1/90, p. 5. The relationship between ancient history and rhetoric has become a hackneyed theme, A. Cameron, in AC, p. 1 and n. 1 (references).

4 M. L. Clarke, *Rhetoric at Rome* (1953), p. 88; cf. p. 158 n. 14.

5 C. Kelly, *Times Literary Supplement* 28/5/93, p. 22, complained that

there was much muddle-headed, half-baked rhetoric in history. The distinction between rhetoric and history sometimes became blurred, PGW, p. 25. Cf. Seneca the elder, *Controversiae*, IX, 6.12, MC, p. 11, HEB, p. 35.

6 R. Brock, op. cit., p. 102.

7 E. Gabba, in MC, p. 59.

8 Polybius, XII, 25a, cf. b, SU, p. 110, HEB, p. 34.

9 Cicero, *On the Orator*, II, 15.62 (tr. H. Rackham and E. W. Sutton); cf. II, 31.64, *Brutus* 42.83, *Orator* 20.66. RMa, p. 19, RMe, p. 113.

10 JBB, p. 226, cf. p. 228, P. G. Walsh, in TAD/*LH*, p. 115, SU, p. 189, C. T. Cruttwell, *A History of Latin Literature* (6th edn, 1898), p. 322.

11 Plutarch, 855E.

12 RS/*TST*, p. 7.

13 E. Aubrion, *Rhétorique et histoire chez Tacite* (1985), H. Bardon, *A propos des Histoires: Tacite et la tentation de la rhétorique*, PP, p. 145 n. 34.

14 J. Cousin, 'Rhetorik und Psychologie des Tacitus', in V. Pöschl (ed.) *Tacitus* (1969), p. 113, B. Walker, *The Annals of Tacitus* (1960), pp. 204ff, RMe, p. 71.

15 RS/*T*, Appendix 69, p. 763.

16 A. Gudeman, quoted by A. H. McDonald, in MP, p. 481.

17 PP, pp. 79, 145 n. 54.

18 M. I. Finley, *History and Theory*, IV, 1965, p. 282.

19 B. Walker, *The Annals of Tacitus* (1960), p. 154 n. 1.

20 CWF, p. 188.

21 H. I. Marrou, in MIF/*LGNA*, pp. 198ff. JP, p. 16, warns that we should not too readily accept the distorting medium of Socratic prejudice against rhetoric; we need not be too sceptical about its influence on history, A. Cameron, in AC, p. 206.

22 PGW, p. 20 n. 2.

23 W. H. Walsh, 'Plato and the Philosophy of History', *History and Theory*, II.1.1962, pp. 3–16.

24 Cicero, *On the Orator*, II, 14.58.

25 M. I. Finley, *History and Theory*, IV, 1965, p. 252.

26 A. Momigliano, in MIF/*LGNA*, p. 163.

27 Plutarch, XII, 24.

28 A. H. McDonald in MP, p. 478, cf. p. 467.

29 P. Levi, *A History of Greek Literature* (1985), p. 477; cf. A. Lesky, *A History of Greek Literature* (1966), p. 823.

30 Yet H. White, *Metahistory: The Historical Imagination in Nineteenth Century Europe* (1973), saw history as partly philosophical, RMe, p. 193 n. 155. For the relation between history and philosophy cf. also RS/*FH*, p. 20. Posidonius was concerned to reunite them. Lord Acton (*Lectures on Modern History* [1906, 1960], p. 35) declared: 'Philosophers claim that, as early as 1804, they began to bow the metaphysical neck beneath the historical yoke.'

History and Documents

1 Cf. MIF/*AH*, Ch. 3 and pp. 11, 15, 114 n. 17, and *History and Theory*, IV, 1965, pp. 292, 296. Polybius, XII, 25e, 7, wrote that one can no more become a historian by studying documents than one can become a painter by looking at old masters, cf. F. W. Walbank, in TAD/*LH*, p. 49. But see P. Fraccaro, *JRS*, LXV, 1956, p. 65.
2 E. Gabba, in MC, p. 45.
3 JBB, pp. 30f.
4 MG/*AH*, p. 115, P. A. Brunt, *Thucydides* (1966), p. xxiv.
5 D. M. Lewis, *Epigraphical Congress (Athens)*, 1982, MIF/*AH*, p. 105.
6 JBB, p. 31.
7 Polybius, XII, 25e, 27a.
8 Polybius, XX, 5–7; cf. M. Feyel, *Polybe et l'histoire de Béotie au 3e siècle avant notre ère* (1942), F. W. Walbank, in TAD/*LH*, p. 53.
9 SU, p. 197, PGW, pp. 31, 112. Cf. Livy VI, 1, on a search for early treaties and laws, attributed to 389 BC. The discovery of the *Annales Maximi* only encouraged historiography after a time, E. Badian, in TAD/*LH*, p. 2; cf. pp. 12, 15, A. H. McDonald, in MP, p. 494.
10 MG/*AH*, p. 176 (references on p. 438 nn. 37, 38), R. M. Ogilvie, *JRS*, XXVIII, 1938, p. 46.
11 G. M. Paul, in TAD/*LH*, p. 104.
12 E. Gabba, *JRS*, XXI, 1981, p. 61.
13 J. Briscoe, in TAD/*L*, p. 11.
14 F. W. Walbank, in TAD/*L*, pp. 63, 69 n. 6; cf. pp. 65, 71 n. 123. He describes Livy's treatment of the (so-called) *S. C. De Bacchanalibus* as still *sub judice*.
15 Livy, VI, 20; cf. J. Briscoe, in TAD/*L*, p. 11.
16 Josephus, *Life*, 65; cf. *Against Apion*, I.9, M. Hadas-Lebel, *Flavius Josephus* (1993), pp. 213f.
17 RS/*T*, pp. 389f.
18 G. B. Townend, in TAD/*LB*, p. 87.
19 Plutarch, *Numa* 1: cf. P. Fraccaro, *JRS*, LXV, 1956, p. 62.
20 CWF, p. 186 and n. 19.
21 K. J. Dover, *History and Theory*, IV, 1965, p. 59.
22 T. B. Jones, *Paths to the Ancient Past* (1967), p. 2.
23 MIF/*AH*, pp. 18f.
24 MG/*AH*, pp. 131, 427 n. 6.
25 Cf. H. Mattingly, *Coins of the Roman Empire in the British Museum*, M. Grant, *Roman Imperial Money, Roman History from Coins* (1958, p. 292 1968), *passim*.

3 SOURCES AND STRANGENESS

Sources and Rumours

1 Cf. MIF/*AH*, p. 10. There is 'no rational correlation between importance and evidence', E. Meyer, in MG/*AH*, p. 8.

2 MC, p. 4.
3 Thucydides, I, 21. But his own account of the Fifty Years before the Peloponnesian War (the Pentekontaetea) has been much criticised, SU, p. 35.
4 Xenophon, *Hellenica*, IV, 8, 1.
5 Polybius, XII, 25–28; cf. SU, p. 104.
6 HEB, p. 57. However, in the first century BC people liked abridged history or 'famous sayings', CWF, p. 191.
7 PGW, pp. 144, 273. For the bewildering variety of Sallust's sources, cf. M. J. Wheeldon, in AC, p. 55.
8 MIF/*AH*, p. 18, J. Briscoe, in TAD/*L*, pp. 5f.
9 SU, p. 179, n. 40.
10 E. Burck, in TAD/*L*, p. 36, J. Briscoe, ibid, p. 9; cf. SU, pp. 180, 197.
11 PGW, pp. 143f; cf. p. 273.
12 Tacitus, *Annals*, IV, 53.2; cf. 1.69.2 (the younger Pliny). For the small amount of Tacitus's research, AM, p. 131.
13 RMa, p. 251 n. 10.
14 J. P. V. D. Balsdon, *JRS*, XXXVI, 1946, p. 170 (on Rome).
15 MIF/*AH*, p. 10.
16 Seneca, *Apocolocyntosis*, 1.1, cf. MIF/*AH*, p. 16.
17 Cf. A. Momigliano, *HHA*, p. 27, SU, p. 28.
18 Herodotus VII, 152.3 etc, MG/*AH*, p. 65. For his successful handling of the oral tradition, AM, p. 129; cf. pp. 213ff.
19 SU, p. 110.
20 R. Brock, *Liverpool Classical Monthly* 16/7/91, p. 99.
21 Thucydides I, 22.
22 FWW, pp. 73ff, SU, p. 109.
23 Tacitus, *Annals*, IV, 11.
24 B. Walker, *The Annals of Tacitus* (1960), p. 42, MC, p. 16, RMe, pp. 37 no. 31, 81.
25 RMe, p. 44 no. 56.
26 F. R. D. Goodyear, *Tacitus* (1970), pp. 31f; cf. SU, p. 234.
27 F. R. D. Goodyear, op. cit., p. 32.
28 RMe, pp. 40 n. 44, 43, 54, 174 n. 44, B. Walker, op. cit., pp. 8, 82ff, 235.
29 F. R. D. Goodyear, op. cit., p. 32, B. Walker, op. cit., pp. 110ff.
30 Cf. now L. Raditsa, *Gallatin Review*, XII, 1, 1992–3, p. 19.
31 MG/*AH*, p. 77, JBB, pp. 81, 90.
32 Polybius, XII, 24, 25a, II, 56.2, JBB, pp. 169, 188, FWW, pp. 44 n. 67, 79.
33 E. Burck, in TAD/*L*, p. 28 n. 17.
34 Josephus, *Against Apion*, 1.7.

Selection

1 H. J. Muller, *The Uses of the Past* (1952), p. 40.
2 L. B. Namier, 'History: Its Subject-Matter and Tastes', *History Today*, 1952, p. 161. Besides 'half of what happened people forget entirely', T. Gifford, *The Cavanaugh Quest* (1976), p. 50.

3 R. Syme, *HHA*, p. 70.
4 SU, p. 17, RMa, p. 36 nn. 30, 39.
5 E. Gabba, in MC, pp. 20, 25.
6 FWW, p. 94.
7 W. E. Thompson, *GHLH*, pp. 122, 124, 131.
8 MG/*AH*, p. 211.
9 M. Hadas-Lebel, *Flavius Josephus* (1993), p. 220.
10 E. Gabba, in MC, pp. 42f.
11 Tacitus, *Annals*, XIII, 51.
12 RS/*T*, p. 305.
13 G. B. Townend, in TAD/*LB*, p. 87.
14 Herodotus, VII.152; cf. IV.96 and W. G. Forrest, *Herodotus*, pp. xxiii, xxvi.
15 SU, pp. 5f. n. 3.
16 JBB, pp. 58, 60.
17 Thucydides II, 5; cf. P. A. Brunt, *Thucydides* (1966), p. xxiii.
18 SU, p. 27, JBB, p. 83.
19 Polybius, II, 56 (attacking Phylarchus).
20 Livy, I, praef; cf. PGW, p. 30.
21 MG/*AH*, pp. 236, 238f.
22 Plutarch, *Demetrius*, 15; MG/*AH*, p. 325.
23 F. R. D. Goodyear, *Tacitus* (1970), p. 32.
24 G. B. Townend, in TAD/*LB*, pp. 91ff.

Speeches, Digressions and Cycles

1 CWF, Ch. IV ('The Speech in Greek and Roman Historiography'), pp. 142–68, RS/*FH*, p. 23.
2 There is no need to 'suspend judgement about battle speeches', CWF, p. 162.
3 SU, p. 195.
4 FWW, pp. 240f.
5 MG/*AH*, p. 42, SU, p. 45.
6 CWF, p. 172.
7 A. Lesky, *A History of Greek Literature* (1966), p. 338.
8 P. A. Brunt, *Thucydides* (1966), p. xxiv. Did Herodotus hear a report of Themistocles's words (8.83.1–2) before the battle of Salamis, CWF, p. 163?
9 Herodotus, I, 29–33: already rejected in antiquity, A. W. Gomme and T. J. Cadoux, *OCD*, p. 999.
10 Thucydides, 1.22 (tr. R. Warner); cf. MG/*AH*, p. 89.
11 P. A. Brunt, *Thucydides* (1966), pp. xxvff.
12 C. W. MacLeod, *Collected Essays* (1983), p. 53.
13 J. Wilson, *Phoenix*, XXXVI, 1982, p. 103.
14 MG/*AH*, p. 88.
15 CWF, pp. 142, 151, 155ff, JBB, p. 109.
16 R. Brock, *Liverpool Classical Monthly*, 1991, p. 98 (quoting A. J. Woodman).

17 FWW, pp. 244ff.

18 FMC, p. 149.

19 JBB, pp. 114, 134, FMC, p. 4, MG/*AH*, p. 85. The speech ignores Pericles's championship of the poor, P. A. Brunt, *Thucydides*, p. xxvi.

20 P. Robinson, *GHLH*, pp. 19f, MIF/*AH*, p. 13, CWF, p. 156, FMC, pp. 17f, JBB, p. 113. Was the Melian situation as Thucydides stated? M. Treu etc, *HHA*, pp. 67, 69.

21 SU, p. 80 n. 24; cf. p. 89.

22 Plato, *Timaeus*, 19C F 4.

23 Polybius, xii, 25b, 1–4 (tr. W. R. Paton).

24 Polybius, xii, 25a (tr. I. Scott-Kilvert); cf. CWF, p. 157, SU, p. 110 n. 5.

25 Polybius, ii, 56, v, 20, F. W. Walbank, in TAD/*LH*, p. 53.

26 FWW, p. 69 n. 11, MIF/*AH*, p. 110.

27 F. W. Walbank, in TAD/*LH*, p. 62 nn. 112, 113. Perhaps he found versions in his sources.

28 Cicero, *On the Orator*, ii, 15.62.

29 T. A. Dorey, in TAD/*LH*, p. 78.

30 RS/*S*, pp. 186, 96 n. 73.

31 PGW, pp. 131, 133, MIF/*AH*, p. 110 n. 13.

32 MG/*AH*, pp. 256, 258.

33 K. Wellesley, *Greece and Rome*, i, 2nd series, 1954, p. 13.

34 *Inscriptiones Latinae Selectae*, 212.

35 Tacitus, *Annals*, xi, 24.

36 K. Wellesley, op. cit., pp. 13–26; cf. RMa, pp. 147, 150, 256, R. H. Martin, in TAD/*T*, p. 146 n. 57.

37 K. Wellesley, op. cit., pp. 13–26, cf. MG/*AH*, p. 292.

38 Cicero, *Orator*, 66; cf. PGW, p. 33.

39 Livy, lx.17.1, PGW, p. 40, MG/*AH*, pp. 319f. His digression on Alexander the Great (ix, 17.3ff) was perhaps a youthful exercise.

40 R. H. Barrow, *Plutarch and His Times* (1967), p. 63.

41 Cf. M. Grant, *The Fall of the Roman Empire* (1976), p. 195 etc.

42 Cf. L. Raditsa, *Gallatin Review*, 12.1.1992–3, I. Berlin, 'Historical Inevitability', in H. Meyerhoff (ed.) *The Philosophy of History in Our Time* (1959), pp. 249ff, P. Geyl, *Debates with Historians* (1962), pp. 277ff, 112ff.

43 R. G. Collingwood, *Essays in the Philosophy of History* (1966), pp. 57–89, F. R. D. Goodyear, *Bulletin of the Institute of Classical Studies* (London), xvii, 1970, pp. 106–16, G. W. Trompf, *The Idea of Historical Recurrences in Western Thought* (1979).

44 Cf. V. J. Hunter, *Past and Process in Herodotus and Thucydides* (1952), p. 167.

45 FWW, p. 142.

46 Tacitus, *Annals*, iii, 55; cf. F. R. D. Goodyear, *Tacitus* (1970), P. Gardiner (ed.) *Theories of History* (1959), pp. 11, 56, 200.

47 HEB, p. 39 etc.

Religion and Portents

1 MG/*AH*, p. 193. And in shaping literature: T. S. Eliot, *Essays Ancient and Modern* (1936).
2 AM, p. 108. Cf. Lord Acton, *Lectures on Modern History*, 1906, 1960, p. 23. On the ancients cf. A. Cameron, in AC, pp. 5ff.
3 Cf. Acton, op. cit., p. 27, on earlier times.
4 HEB, p. 29, CWF, pp. 78ff, SU, pp. 19f.
5 JBB, p. 49; cf. p. 47.
6 MG/*AH*, pp. 53f.
7 Herodotus, VIII, 77, cf. SU, pp. 18ff.
8 J. Kirchberg, *Die Funktion der Orakel im Werke Herodots* (1965), pp. 116–20, C. Dewald, *GHLH*, p. 50.
9 Cf. PP, p. 67, A. Lesky, *A History of Greek Literature* (1966), p. 338.
10 Cf. MG/*AH*, p. 55.
11 A. Momigliano, in MIF/*LGNA*, pp. 162f.
12 Polybius, XII, 245; FWW, p. 185.
13 PGW, pp. 68, 48.
14 SU, pp. 118f.
15 Cicero, *On the Orator*, II.63, *Letters to Friends*, v, 12 etc.
16 F. W. Walbank, in TAD/*LH*, p. 60.
17 PGW, pp. 49, 120.
18 P. G. Walsh, in MG/*AH*, p. 241.
19 SU, p. 173 n. 19.
20 Livy, I, 4, cf. JP, pp. 4, 3.
21 MG/*AH*, p. 262.
22 RMe, p. 49.
23 Tertullian in D. R. Dudley, *The World of Tacitus* (1968), p. 237.
24 E. A. Thompson, in TAD/*LH*, p. 151.

Too Little Economic and Social History

1 W. H. B. Court, 'Economic History', in H. P. R. Finberg (ed.) *Approaches to History* (1965), pp. 17–50, M. I. Finley, *The Ancient Economy* (new edn, 1985), JBB, p. 92, A. S. L. Bullock in H. Meyerhoff (ed.) *The Philosophy of History in Our Time* (1959), p. 296, A. Cameron, in AC, p. 3.
2 A. H. M. Jones, *Ancient Economic History* (1948), MIF/*AH*, p. 27.
3 E. Gabba, in MC, p. 23.
4 MG/*AH*, p. 114.
5 P. A. Brunt, *Thucydides* (1966), p. xxiv, JBB, p. 56.
6 PGW, p. 34, P. G. Walsh, in TAD/*LH*, p. 117 and n. 9.
7 MIF/*AH*, p. 4. But see MG/*AH*, p. 235.
8 MC, p. 23.
9 B. Walker, *The Annals of Tacitus* (1960), p. 141.
10 P. Garnsey and R. Saller, *The Roman Empire: Economy, Society and Culture* (1987), p. 43.
11 J. Wacher, in J. Wacher (ed.) *The Roman World*, I, 1987, p. 8. See also

G. M. Trevelyan, *English Social History* (1994), p. vii, A. L. Rowse, *The Use of History* (1946), p. 69, K. R. Popper in P. Gardiner (ed.) *Theories of History* (1959), pp. 276.

12 H. J. Perkin in H. P. R. Finberg (ed.) op. cit., pp. 51–82. Much of this development is due to the French *Annales* historians, who saw events as crests upon the waves of deeper social forces: cf. R. Aron, *History and Theory*, I, 1960, p. 103. Anthropology also plays a large part (MIF/UAH, pp. 102–19), stimulated by structuralism, A. Cameron, in AC, pp. 3f.

13 RMe, p. 164; cf. p. 57.

14 Ammianus Marcellinus, XIV, 6.25: MG/*AH*, pp. 376f.

4 MISINFORMATION AND MISTAKES

Love of a Story

1 Arrian, *Anabasis*, praef.1.3; G. T. Griffith, in MP, p. 184. For story-telling in general, cf. W. J. T. Mitchell (ed.) *On Narrative* (1981), and R. Scholes and R. Kellogg, *The Nature of Narrative* (1976), M. Mandelbaum, 'A Note on History as Narrative', *History and Theory*, VI, 1967, pp. 413–19.

2 CWF, p. 165.

3 R. Ullmann, *Transactions of the American Philological Association*, LXXIII, 1942, p. 27.

4 MG/*AH*, pp. 59f.

5 Ibid, p. 52.

6 JBB, pp. 57, 60.

7 M. I. Finley, *The Greek Historians* (1959), p. 6.

8 G. T. Griffith, in MP, p. 198, RS/*FH*, p. 3.

9 F. W. Walbank, in TAD/*LH*, p. 46.

10 Tacitus, *Annals*, IV, 11; cf. RMe, pp. 37, 257 n. 31 etc.

Self-Justification

1 C. Kelly, *Times Literary Supplement* 28/5/93, p. 22, speaks of 'wounded pride'.

2 MIF/*AH*, p. 51.

3 Solon, 32–40 (36.5–7).

4 Thucydides, IV, 106, v.26; JP; p. 8.

5 Marcellinus, *Life of Thucydides*, 46.

6 MG/*AH*, pp. 98, 116f, J. B. Bury and R. Meiggs, *A History of Greece* (4th edn, 1975), p. 280.

7 Thucydides, III.366, IV.27.3, 28.5–4, 5.12–13, 161; G. T. Griffith, in MP, p. 192, A. G. Woodhead, 'Thucydides's Portrait of Cleon', *Mnemosyne* XIII, 1960, pp. 289–317.

8 J. H. Finley, *Three Essays on Thucydides* (1967), p. xi.

9 E.g. Dionysius of Halicarnassus, *Letter to Pompeius*, 3.9; cf. JBB, pp. 131f, M. I. Finley, *JRS*, LXXIII, 1983, p. 39, MG/*AH*, p. 117.

10 C. Grayson, in B. Levick (ed.) *The Ancient Historian and his Materials* (1975), pp. 31f.

11 SU, p. 175.

12 CWF, p. 180.

13 F. W. Walbank, in TAD/*LH*, p. 54.

14 E. Badian, ibid, p. 13.

15 Cicero, *To His Friends*, v.8; cf. MG/*AH*, pp. 175, 438 n. 31.

16 Cicero, *op. cit.*, v.12.3 (tr. W. G. Williams).

17 JBB, p. 233, SU, p. 139, MG/*AH*, pp. 186, 190, T. A. Dorey, in TAD/*LH*, p. 74, F. E. Adcock, *Caesar as Man of Letters* (1956), pp. 22ff.

18 RS/*S*, p. 256, G. M. Paul, in TAD/*LH*, pp. 86–90, E. Badian, in TAD/*LH*, p. 24, MG/*AH*, p. 199.

19 Macrobius, *Saturnalia*, I, 11 (2), Cicero, *Philippics*, XII, 10.

20 M. Hadas-Lebel, *Flavius Josephus* (1993), p. 213, MG/*AH*, pp. 251, 264–7, MC, p. 19.

21 RMa, p. 28, B. Walker, *The Annals of Tacitus* (1960), pp. 173–81, 188, 257.

22 RMe, pp. 85f; cf. pp. 9, 166.

23 SU, p. 253.

Influences

1 RMe, p. 178 n. 32, E. Badian, in TAD/*LH*, p. 28 n. 2.

2 CWF, pp. 5f, 12.

3 F. M. Cornford, *Thucydides Mythistoricus* (1907, 1965), pp. 245f.

4 MIF/*AH*, p. 17, RMe, p. 51.

5 CWF, p. 53.

6 Cicero, *Brutus*, 62.

7 PGW, pp. 152f, 89.

8 Ibid, pp. 145, 146, J. Briscoe, in TAD/*LH*, pp. 3f.

9 Cf. D. R. Dudley, *The World of Tacitus* (1968), p. 242 n. 3.

10 RS/*T*, pp. 562–3, RMa, p. 48, RMe, p. 105.

11 MG/*AH*, p. 113. 'There is no such thing as politically innocent historiography', H. White, in H. White and F. E. Manuel (eds) *Theories of History* (1978), p. 20. But cf. PP, p. 13 (blurb): 'what is historically false can be politically true'; and D. Edgar, *Sunday Telegraph* 22/8/93, p. 9: 'The failure to distinguish between literal and metaphorical truth has entered political discourse.'

12 Discussed at length by Plutarch, *On the Malice of Herodotus*, 168F, 858, 27.862F, 863A; cf. JBB, p. 64 and n. 7.

13 Plutarch, *op. cit.*, 40, 871C, JBB, p. 64 n. 3.

14 MG/*AH*, p. 114. Thus, Thucydides passes over the role of the mercantile middle class in prompting the Peloponnesian War, omits the raising of the tribute in 414 (JBB, p. 86), and neglects the Megarian decree (cf. p. 77). For his views on the meaning of power, A. G. Woodhead,

Thucydides on the Nature of Power (1970), K. J. Dover, *Thucydides* (1973), p. 41.

15 HEB, pp. 31f.

16 CWF, p. 97, SU, p. 34.

17 JBB, pp. 152f, SU, pp. 92, 109.

18 FWW, p. 177 n. 122 (reservations), F. W. Walbank, in TAD/*LH*, p. 53, *American Journal of Philology*, LVI, 1940, pp. 129–65, SU, p. 111.

19 Polybius, VIII.9–11; cf. FWW, pp. 40, 49. Histories of cities tended to attack monarchies.

20 FWW, p. 8. Yet Polybius attacks Fabius Pictor (p. 113) for his senatorial bias.

21 RS/*S*, p. 186 and n. 37.

22 Theory and practice do not always coincide: T. P. Wiseman, *History*, LXVI, 1981, pp. 375–93, A. J. Woodman, *Bulletin of the Council of University Classics Departments*, VII, 1978, pp. 6ff.

23 Cicero, *Laws*, 1.4; cf. CWF, p. 135, G. M. Townend, in T. A. Dorey (ed.) *Cicero* (1964), p. 121, J. de R. Evans, *The Art of Persuasion: Political Propaganda from Aeneas to Brutus* (1992).

24 Posidonius was too partial to him, JBB, p. 221.

25 G. M. Paul, in TAD/*LH*, p. 90, cf. p. 98, RS/*S*, pp. 367f, 125. But Sallust did not care either for the senate's political enemies, the *populares*, G. M. Paul, op. cit., p. 101. He lapsed from partisanship for Caesar, RS/*S*, p. 286.

26 SU, p. 152 and n. 33.

27 E. Burck, in TAD/*L*, p. 34.

28 P. G. Walsh, in TAD/*LH*, p. 118; cf. E. Gabba in F. Millar and E. Segal (eds) *Caesar Augustus: Seven Aspects* (1984), pp. 61–88. It seems possible that Livy terminated his history when he did (in 9BC) because of his ambivalent view; but this is contested, J. Henderson, in AC, pp. 64, 73f. The speech of Marcus Furius Camillus (v.51–54) perhaps represents Livy's own opinions on contemporary affairs. R. M. Ogilvie, *A Commentary on Livy: Books 1–5* (1965), p. 742.

29 RMe, p. 89. The traditional pattern envisaged good reigns deteriorating into tyranny, RMa, p. 187.

30 E. A. Thompson, in TAD/*LH*, p. 148 and n. 10.

31 H. Pirenne, *Revue historique* (1897), p. 51, G. J. Renier, *History: Its Purpose and Method* (1950, 1982), p. 250.

32 JBB, p. 252.

33 E. Meyer: 'the function of history is the elucidation of the present'; C. Beard, 'That Noble Dream', (*American Historical Review*, October 1935): 'each historian who writes history is the product of his age'; cf. MIF/*AH*, pp. 4, 86.

34 C. Beard, op. cit., CWF, pp. 197f.

35 R. Syme, *HHA*, p. 29, CWF, p. 105.

36 MG/*AH*, p. 85. The speech of Hermocrates is another anachronism, P. A. Brunt, *Thucydides* (1966), p. xxxii.

37 Polybius, XII, 256 (tr. R. Paton).

38 RS/*S*, p. 186 and n. 33, A. H. McDonald, in MP, p. 473; though Sallust

did not have a very good understanding of the politics of his own day, HEB, p. 37.

39 G. M. Paul, in TAD/*L*, p. 90.
40 J. Briscoe, ibid, p. 9.
41 MG/*AH*, p. 325.
42 Discussed by F. R. D. Goodyear, *Tacitus* (1970), p. 20.

Chauvinism

1 FJT, p. 38, cf. p. 28.
2 Lucian, *On Writing History*, 41.
3 A. Momigliano, in MIF/*LGNA*, p. 165.
4 SU, p. 12, W. G. Forrest, *Herodotus*, p. xxiv. Plutarch, *On the Malice of Herodotus*, 12.857A, criticised him as a lover of barbarians.
5 D. M. Lewis, *GHLH*, pp. 102, 107f.
6 Herodotus, VII, 139; JBB, pp. 63ff, MG/*AH*, p. 93.
7 Plutarch, op. cit., 1.854F, 31.864D.
8 P. A. Brunt, *Thucydides* (1966), pp. xxvii, xxxi.
9 MG/*AH*, p. 390.
10 Ibid, p. 115.
11 S. W. Hirsch, *GHLH*, p. 66.
12 SU, p. 93. Thus, he omits the important 'general peace' (*koine eirene*), G. T. Griffith, in MP, p. 197.
13 SU, pp. 92ff, W. P. Henry, *Greek Historical Writing* (1966), p. 206.
14 Plato, *Republic*, III, 21, 414 B-C.
15 F. W. Walbank, in TAD/*AH*, p. 53. Polybius had been chosen to carry the ashes of the Achaean leader Philopoemen.
16 See Phylarchus, Theopompus, Ephorus and Postumius Albinus, pp. 111, 109, 108, 113.
17 FWW, pp. 4, 46 n. 74, 165. He attacked Antisthenes for what he regarded as absurd anti-Roman slanders.
18 Polybius, I, 65.7, FWW, p. 89 n. 144.
19 E.g. Livy, 5, P. G. Walsh, in TAD/*LH*, p. 133 (responsibility of Hannibal).
20 RS/*S*, p. 249 n. 58, SU, p. 144.
21 HEB, p. 37, FJT, p. 27, J. H. Whitfield, in TAD/*L*, p. 37.
22 PGW, pp. 36, 151ff.
23 P. G. Walsh, in TAD/*LH*, pp. 115, 126 n. 62.
24 Livy, I.1 (tr. A. Selincourt).
25 P. G. Walsh, op. cit., p. 132 nn. 9ff.
26 E. Burck, ibid, pp. 30ff.
27 PGW, p. 153.
28 P. G. Walsh, in TAD/*LH*, pp. 128, 140 n. 71.
29 F. W. Walbank, ibid, pp. 57, 55.
30 A. H. McDonald, in MP, p. 479 (references).
31 HEB, p. 24.
32 MC, p. 16, MG/*AH*, p. 268.
33 D. R. Dudley, *The World of Tacitus* (1968), p. 196.

34 MG/*AH*, p. 326. But Plutarch did not indulge in national bias or flattery.
35 Ibid, p. 311.
36 Ibid, p. 312; cf. p. 406.
37 RS/*TST*, p. 9.
38 F. R. D. Goodyear, *Tacitus* (1970), p. 8.
39 SU, p. 256.
40 CWF, p. 56.
41 Tacitus, *Annals*, I, 1.
42 JBB, p. 234, RS/*TST*, p. 9.
43 RMe, p. 164, RS/*T*, pp. 443ff. References in K. Wellesley, in TAD/*T*, p. 95 n. 1.
44 MG/*AH*, p. 329.
45 A. Momigliano, MIF/*LGNA*, p. 159.
46 Herodotus, III, 115, MG/*AH*, p. 65. P. Adams, *Travelers and Travel Liars* (1980), would not have surprised him. For Herodotus's conscientiousness about geography (inherited from Hecataeus), cf. AM, p. 211.
47 Thucydides, I.20, I.97; cf. JBB, p. 90.
48 JBB, p. 86 n. 1: or partly due to a scribe?
49 Polybius, XII, 25e.1.
50 Ibid, 79.7f.
51 FWW, p. 128 and n. 66.
52 W. E. Thompson, *GHLH*, p. 121.
53 FWW, p. 118 and n. 112, G. T. Griffith, in MP, p. 202 n. 93.
54 Cicero, *On the Orator*, II.63, *Orator* 66.
55 A. J. Woodman, *Rhetoric in Classical Historiography: Four Studies* (1988), pp. 114f.
56 A. H. McDonald, in MP, p. 475, C. T. Cruttwell, *A History of Roman Literature* (6th edn, 1898), pp. 191ff.
57 A. J. Woodman, op. cit., p. 114.
58 Ibid, MG/*AH*, p. 256.
59 Strabo, II, 1, 9c.70.
60 D. R. Dudley, *The World of Tacitus* (1968), p. 178. Cf. RS/*T*, pp. 39f n. 5, on the Brigantes. Tacitus was also wrong about Castra Vetera, RMe, pp. 173f n. 39. Cf. also K. Wellesley, in TAD/*LH*, p. 77.
61 RS/*T*, p. 396.
62 SU, p. 216.
63 D. R. Dudley, op. cit., pp. 174ff (Ch. 4: The Provinces).
64 A. Wallace-Hadrill, in W. Hamilton and A. Wallace-Hadrill, *Ammianus Marcellinus: The Later Roman Empire (AD 354–378)* (1986), p. 29.

Wars

1 Cf. A. J. Woodman, 'From Hannibal to Hitler: The Literature of War', *University of Leeds Journal*, 1983, p. 121; cf. R. Brock, *Liverpool Classical Monthly* 16/7/91, p. 100. On the causes of ancient wars, as described, cf. AM, Ch. 7, pp. 112–26.
2 MIF/*AH*, pp. 70, 106.

3 FJT, p. 22, W. G. Forrest, *Herodotus*, p. xxiv.
4 *CWF*, p. 162, is too kind in saying one must 'suspend judgement' about some of them.
5 G. T. Griffith, in MP, p. 187, W. G. Forrest, *Herodotus*, p. xxi, JBB, pp. 71f. Nevertheless, Herodotus was the first to organise a large-scale enquiry about a war and its causes, AM, p. 116.
6 Thucydides, i, 2.1.
7 SU, p. 24.
8 Ibid, p. 41.
9 JBB, p. 87 n. 1; cf. FMC, pp. 25–38.
10 MG/*AH*, p. 131 n. 18; on Xenophon and the battle of Cunaxa, G. Wylie, *L'Antiquité Classique* (1992), pp. 80–97.
11 Polybius, xii, 25h.
12 FWW, pp. 88ff. Yet Polybius taught historians to distinguish between the remote and immediate causes of wars, AM, p. 124.
13 RS/S, p. 147. However, it has been suggested that this is the only impressive Roman account of the origins of a war, AM, p. 121.
14 Cicero, *On the Orator*, ii, 15.62.
15 F. E. Adcock, *Caesar as Man of Letters* (1956), p. 22.
16 JP, p. 12.
17 PGW, pp. 157ff; cf. pp. 35, 279ff, SU, p. 171, J. Briscoe, in TAD/*L*, p. 7 n. 26, P. G. Walsh, ibid, pp. 186f.
18 PGW, p. 285.
19 JP, pp. 7f.
20 RMe, pp. 157 (cf. p. 31), 174.
21 D. R. Dudley, *The World of Tacitus* (1968), p. 178, K. Wellesley, in TAD/*LH*, p. 71 (cf. p. 63).
22 RMe, pp. 38f.
23 T. Mommsen, *The Provinces of the Roman Empire* (1886), i, p. 181.
24 RS/*T*, pp. 392ff.
25 Ibid, p. 395 (Appendix 64).
26 JP, p. 10.
27 RMe, pp. 157, 174.
28 For his attitude in the confused situation, see A. Momigliano, *Cambridge Ancient History*, x, 1934, p. 858.

Biography

1 M. Grant, *Gallatin Review*, xii, 1, 1992–3, p. 59.
2 R. G. Collingwood, *Essays in the Philosophy of History* (1966), pp. 134–8, JBB, p. 212.
3 Seneca the younger, *Apocolocyntosis*, 1.1; cf. JBB, p. 154.
4 Lucian, *On Writing History*, 7, CWE, p. 189. 'Guard against the prestige of great names,' said Lord Acton, *Lectures on Modern History*, 1906, 1960, p. 37. M. F. Lefkowitz, *The Lives of the Greek Poets*, p. 99, points out that the 'lives' of poets are often derived from their own works.
5 Is psychological history really history at all? RMe, p. 177 n. 9.

6 JBB, p. 57 n. 1, SU, pp. 16f.

7 JBB, pp. 146f, HEB, p. 32.

8 SU, p. 99.

9 Ibid, pp. 67f, 71, 82f, J. K. Anderson, *Xenophon* (1974), pp. 167f.

10 JBB, pp. 138f, 153, PGW, p. 25 n. 3. This tendency was much encouraged by the more or less fictional writings about Alexander the Great, R. Stoneman (ed.) *The Greek Alexander Romances* (1991).

11 Polybius, XII, 25.2, XVI, 14.6–10, etc, F. W. Walbank, in TAD/*LH*, p. 52 nn. 99, 100.

12 SU, pp. 112, 115, FWW, p. 96, CWF, p. 113.

13 Polybius, I, 14 (tr. E. Badian).

14 Cicero, *Brutus*, 11.44, *On the Orator*, II.15.6, *Laws*, I.34, CWF, p. 104 n. 17. For ancient autobiographies cf. G. Misch, *A History of Autobiography in Antiquity* (2 vols, 1950).

15 RS/*S*, p. 117, cf. pp. 205, 526, SU, pp. 149f, MG/*AH*, p. 208.

16 F. W. Walbank, in TAD/*LH*, p. 53, P. G. Walsh, ibid, p. 139.

17 MC, p. 10, CWF, p. 65.

18 H. J. Muller, *The Uses of the Past* (1952), pp. 47, 274.

19 RS/*TST*, p. 120.

20 M. Hadas-Lebel, *Flavius Josephus* (1993), p. 213.

21 MG/*AH*, p. 256.

22 F. R. D. Goodyear, *Tacitus* (1970), p. 33.

23 SU, p. 214, RMa, p. 109: A. H. McDonald, in MP, p. 480, RS/*T*, pp. 387, 419 n. 3, 420–34, RMe, pp. 25, 42, 73, 86, 92.

24 RMe, p. 24 n. 88.

25 RS/*T*, p. 364, SU, pp. 204 n. 1, 208 n. 6, F. R. D. Goodyear, op. cit., p. 29.

26 Tacitus, *Histories*, I, 1; cf. RMe, p. 35 n. 26.

27 RMa, pp. 150, 161.

28 D. R. Dudley, *The World of Tacitus* (1968), p. 106, RMa, pp. 161, 176f, 145, 160f.

29 RS/*T*, p. 419, A. H. McDonald, in MP, pp. 48f.

30 M. Hadas, *A History of Latin Literature* (1952), p. 332.

31 P. Levi, *A History of Greek Literature* (1985), p. 471.

32 Plutarch, *Alexander*, 1.2, CWF, p. 185.

33 A. Lesky, *A History of Greek Literature* (1966), p. 824. There was much attention to physiognomy, now fashionable, PP, pp. 79, 145 n. 54.

34 C. P. Jones, *Plutarch and Rome* (1971), p. 101; cf. p. 89.

35 A. J. Gossage, in TAD/*LB*, p. 63.

36 CWF, p. 188, SU, p. 257.

37 E. A. Thompson, in TAD/*LH*, pp. 145f, SU, p. 253.

38 E. A. Thompson, op. cit., p. 148 and n. 10.

39 MG/*AH*, p. 363.

Moralising

1 Cf. H. Butterfield, 'History and Morality', in H. Meyerhoff (ed.), *The Philosophy of History in Our Time* (1959), pp. 225–49.

2 RMe, p. 31.

3 Lord Acton, *Lectures on Modern History*, 1906, 1960, p. 41.

4 Cf. H. White, in W. J. T. Mitchell (ed.) *On Narrative* (1981), p. 23: 'Could we even narrativise *without* moralising?' Gordon Wright, in his 1975 Presidential Address to the American Historical Association, suggested that our search for the truth needs 'commitment to some deeply held humane values'. Cf. M. Grant, *Ancient History* (1952), p. 26, H. J. Muller, *The Uses of the Past* (1952), p. 41.

5 E.g. Anatole France, *La vie littéraire*, I, p. 244.

6 J. R. M. Butler, in M. Grant, op. cit., p. 151.

7 Cf. discussion on 'Bias in Historical Writing', *History*, October 1926; M. I. Finley, *JRS*, LXXXIII, 1993, p. 31.

8 Aeschylus moralised mythology, JBB, p. 21.

9 RMe, p. 47.

10 D. Lateiner, *GHLH*, p. 96. Herodotus moralised divine disapproval (*phthonos*), H. Lloyd-Jones, *The Justice of Zeus* (1971), p. 69 n. 244.

11 The moral attitude of Thucydides presents a problem, K. J. Dover, *Thucydides*, 1973, pp. 35f.

12 C. Grayson, in B. Levick (ed.) *The Ancient Historian and his Materials* (1975), pp. 31, 37f, JBB, p. 153.

13 CWF, p. 107.

14 Ibid, p. 113, FWW, pp. 213, 223.

15 FWW, p. 86.

16 F. W. Walbank, in TAD/*LH*, pp. 44, 57.

17 G. M. Paul, in TAD/*LH*, p. 93, CWF, p. 72 n. 30, MG/*AH*, pp. 207, 209, SU, p. 143.

18 PGW, pp. 66, 80, 88, SU, p. 167 and n. 3.

19 Livy I, praef., JP, p. 12.

20 E. Gabba, in MC, pp. 17f.

21 Oliver Goldsmith, *Miscellaneous Essays* (1765), No. 13: cf. A. J. Gossage, in TAD/*LB*, pp. 65f.

22 J. B. V. D. Balsdon, *JRS*, XXXVI, 1946, p. 50; cf. Tertullian, *Apologeticus*, XVI, who called him an articulate liar.

Error

1 A. J. Woodman, 'From Hannibal to Hitler: The Literature of War', *University of Leeds Journal*, 1983, p. 112, gives a modern example (Sir Edmund Backhouse).

2 M. I. Finley, *History and Theory*, IV, 1965, p. 148. For eighteenth-century lists of ancient errors, AM, p. 36 n. 33.

3 Plutarch, *On the Malice of Herodotus, passim*. Herodotus came in for a good deal of ancient criticism; cf. Cicero, *Laws*, I.1.5, *On Divination*, II, 116; cf. AM, pp. 128, 131, 133.

4 MG/*AH*, pp. 64 n. 35, 165.
5 K. J. Dover, *History and Theory*, IV, 1965, p. 63.
6 V. J. Hunter, *Past and Process in Herodotus and Thucydides* (1982), K. J. Dover, op. cit., p. 61.
7 SU, p. 26.
8 Ibid, p. 86; C. Grayson, in B. Levick (ed.), *The Ancient Historian and his Materials* (1975), pp. 31f, W. P. Henry, *Greek Historical Writing* (1966), pp. 1f; cf. p. 192.
9 M. M. Gwyn, *Historia*, XXXIX, 1990, pp. 37–76, FWW, p. 40 n. 74, G. T. Griffith, in MP, pp. 202 nn. 91, 93.
10 Suetonius, *Caesar*, 56, cf. CWF, p. 61, SU, p. 138. Cicero had accused Clitarchus and Stratocles of inventions, *Brutus*, 11.44, CWF, p. 136. The later 'annalists' went in for falsification a great deal, MG/*AH*, p. 176.
11 RS/*S*, pp. 96f, 101f, 136, 142. Other mistakes are listed on pp. 74f. For Sallust's political errors see pp. 67, 69.
12 RS/*S*, pp. 72, 77, 82.
13 E.g. J. Briscoe, in TAD/*L*, p. 9, E. Burck, ibid, pp. 36ff.
14 Suetonius, *Gaius*, 34, Quintilian, x.1.32.
15 Dante, *Inferno*, XXVIII, 10.
16 Tacitus, *Histories*, I, 1.
17 RMe, p. 38, 85 n. 65, RS/*T*, Ch. 29 ('The Accuracy of Tacitus').
18 RMe, p. 21, A. J. Woodman, *Rhetoric in Classical Historiography: Four Studies* (1988), pp. 117ff.
19 RS/*T*, pp. 746ff (Appendix 61).
20 F. R. D. Goodyear, *Tacitus* (1970), pp. 18f, RMe, p. 40.
21 A. J. Gossage, in TAD/*LB*, pp. 64f.
22 G. B. Townend, ibid, pp. 91, 95, PP, pp. 19, 69.

5 SHOULD WE READ THE ANCIENT HISTORIANS?

Fact and Fiction

1 On 'metahistory' see H. White, *Metahistory: The Historical Imagination in Nineteenth Century Europe* (1973). The term 'meta-fiction' has also been used, cf. P. Waugh, *Metafiction*, 1984. For the first uses of *mythistoria* and *mythistoricus* cf. RS/*FH*, p. 24. On modernist and post-modernist concepts of historical objectivity and relativism cf. *The Times Literary Supplement* 16/8/92, p. 12. Do not trust any historian, says R. Shenkman, *Legends, Lies and Cherished Myths of World History* (1993), p. 3.
2 John, 18.37f; cf. JP, pp. 1ff, A. Cameron, in AC, pp. 5ff, on Christian 'truth'.
3 R. Bruce-Lockhart, *History Today*, XLIII, August 1993, p. 9.
4 J. Barzun, *Proceedings of the Massachusetts Historical Society*, XCV, 1983, p. 148.
5 With the help of documents (pp. 118–22): Lord Acton, *Lectures on Modern History*, 1906, 1960, p. 23; cf. p. 41.

6 Discussed by MIF/*AH*, pp. 47–66, MIF/*UAH*, p. 29. For discussion about whether history can, or should, be called a 'science': J. L. Gorman, *History and Theory* (1987), pp. 100f.

7 AM, p. 105: cf. C. L. Becker, 'What are Historical Facts?', *Western Political Quarterly*, VIII, 3/9/55, pp. 327–40. D. Edgar, *Sunday Times* 22/8/93, p. 9, wrote: 'To judge fiction as fact denies human beings a unique and effective means of comprehending the real world.' On the distinction between history and fiction, M. J. Wheeldon, in AC, pp. 33, 36, R. Scholes, in W. J. T. Mitchell (ed.) *On Narrative* (1981), p. 207; for a more sceptical view, H. White, *Topics of Discourse* (1978), p. 82.

8 JBB, p. 107.

9 MIF/*AH*, p. 6, A. Bullock, in H. Meyerhoff (ed.) *The Philosophy of History in Our Time* (1959), p. 295. Generalisations are also necessary, MIF/*UAH*, pp. 60–74. Should, or can, a historian avoid offering judgements? C. G. Starr, in H. Temporini (ed.) *Aufstieg und Niedergang der römischen Welt*, I, 1, 1972, pp. 3–11.

10 K. J. Dover, *Thucydides* (1973), p. 5.

11 JBB, p. 252.

12 R. G. Collingwood, *The Idea of History* (1946), p. 248.

13 H. J. Muller, *The Uses of the Past* (1952), p. 44.

14 MIF/*AH*, p. 2.

15 Cf. MG/*AH*, p. 17, and quotations there.

16 Cf. now RMe, p. 39; L. B. Namier, *History Today*, 1952, p. 161. A historian's aim is to know himself, T. A. Dorey, in TAD/*LH*, p. ix.

17 R. Pirenne, *Revue historique* (1897), p. 51.

18 RMa, p. 242, and quotations there.

19 C. Beard, *The Noble Dream* (1935), quoted by CWF, pp. 197f.

20 Discussed by H. J. Muller, *The Uses of the Past* (1952), p. 42.

21 Ibid, p. 44.

22 G. J. Renier, *History: Its Purpose and Method* (1950), p. 250.

23 Cf. pp. 42–4, 90–7.

24 V. Glendinning, *The Grown-Ups* (1989), p. 4.

25 E. Gabba, in MC, p. 25.

26 G. J. Renier, op. cit., p. 249.

27 W. Bauer, *Einführung in das Studium der Geschichte* (1928), p. 89.

28 Seneca the younger, *Apocolocyntosis*, 1.1; cf. F. R. D. Goodyear, *Tacitus* (1970), p. 29.

29 Lucian, *On the Writing of History*, 30; AM, p. 216.

30 MIF/*AH*, p. 13.

31 Ibid, pp. 9, 13, CWF, pp. 9f.

32 CWF, p. 135.

33 T. B. Jones, *Paths to the Ancient Past* (1967), p. 70.

34 RMe, p. 56.

35 Lucian, op. cit., 51.

36 JP, p. 5.

37 MIF/*AH*, pp. 10, 12.

38 Herodotus, I.5, III.122; SU, pp. 5f, JBB, p. 46.

39 Thucydides, I, 21F; SU, p. 29 n. 2, HEB, p. 30, P. A. Brunt, *Thucydides* (1966), p. xxix.

40 P. Robinson, *GHLH*, pp. 19, 23 (cf. R. G. Collingwood, *The Idea of History*).
41 J. K. Anderson, *Xenophon* (1974), p. 84, HEB, p. 34.
42 FJT, p. 57.
43 CWF, p. 98 n. 8.
44 JBB, p. 175, PGW, pp. 27, 49.
45 Polybius, xii, 256, ii.56.2, 10f, SU, p. 12 and n. 6, MG/*AH*, pp. 159, 164.
46 FWW, p. 30.
47 Polybius, iii.31 (tr. E. Badian).
48 Cicero, *On the Orator*, ii, 62, *Laws*, i.6; but see PGW, p. 33 n. 4.
49 Sallust, *Catiline*, 3, 2; RS/S, pp. 83, 248 n. 49.
50 P. G. Walsh, in TAD/*LH*, p. 119.
51 Livy, i, 1. Livy's talent is mainly non-historical, PGW, p. 21. See also J. Henderson, 'Livy and the Invention of History', in AC, pp. 66–85.
52 Plutarch, *On the Glory of the Athenians*, 347a, *On the Malice of Herodotus, passim*.
53 RMe, p. 129, F. R. D. Goodyear, *Tacitus* (1970), p. 44.
54 G. J. Renier, *History: Its Purpose and Method* (1950, 1982), p. 44. The distinction between Tacitus the historian and Tacitus the literary artist is blurred, F. R. D. Goodyear, op. cit., pp. 34–43.

Literary Excellence

1 Discussed by C. Murray, in AC, pp. 163–80.
2 RMe, pp. 136f. The career of Alexander the Great encouraged the growth of the historical romance, SU, p. 105, cf. pp. 80–4 this volume. Yet comparison of history with the historical novel, though tempting, is wrong, JP, pp. 8f.
3 SU, p. x.
4 M. Grant, *A Short History of Classical Civilisation (The Founders of the Western World)*, 1991, pp. 1f, *Gallatin Review*, 12, 1, 1992/3, pp. 57–65.
5 A. J. Woodman, *University of Leeds Journal*, 1983, p. 120, RMe, p. 136. Cf. H. White, *Topics of Discourse* (1978), p. 82: historical narratives are closer to literature than to science. See also A. Cameron, in AC, p. 8, cf. p. 2.
6 JP, pp. 10f.
7 F. Harrison, *The Meaning of History* (1894), p. 8.
8 Lucian, *On Writing History*, 34.
9 F. R. D. Goodyear, *Tacitus* (1970), p. 34.
10 Cf. RMe, p. 136.
11 C. T. Cruttwell, *A History of Roman Literature* (6th edn, 1898), p. 188.
12 PP, p. 155 n. 19.
13 SU, p. ix.

6 OTHER SOURCES OF INFORMATION

Other Historians

1 P. Levi, *A History of Greek Literature* (1985), pp. 307f.
2 JP, p. 16 (exceptions).
3 SU, pp. 236 nn. 1, 2, 237.
4 Diodorus, xx, 1, 2.
5 Diodorus, ibid (tr. C. H. Oldfather); CWF, pp. 147f.
6 MIF/*AH*, pp. 37, 47.
7 M. Fox, *JRS*, LXXXIII, 1993, p. 38.
8 MC, p. 18; cf. p. 12.
9 MIF/*AH*, p. 30.
10 Ibid, p. 33.
11 M. Fox, op. cit., p. 41.
12 SU, p. 240; cf. MC, p. 6.
13 MIF/*AH*, pp. 13f; cf. FMC, p. 180. On the Alban Wars he echoes Thucydides. Dionysius admires Herodotus but is silent about his veracity, AM, p. 134.
14 A. Momigliano, in MIF/*LGNA*, p. 156.
15 *OCD*, p. 728.
16 Nepos, *Pelopidas*, 1; cf. E. I. McQueen, in TAD/*LB*, p. 17.
17 E. Jenkinson, in TAD/*LB*, pp. 10f.
18 Pliny the elder, *Natural History*, v, 1, 4.
19 CWF, pp. 58f, MG/*AH*, p. 177.
20 E. S. Forster and G. B. Townend, *OCD*, p. 1112. Turgid rhetoric, RMa, p. 246 n. 30.
21 RS/*TST*, p. 121. See also A. J. Woodman, *Velleius Paterculus: The Tiberian Narrative* (1971), *Velleius Paterculus: The Caesarian and Augustan Narrative* (1991).
22 RMa, p. 246 n. 30.
23 E. Jenkinson, in TAD/*LB*, p. 5; cf. E. I. McQueen, ibid, pp. 17f.
24 E. Jenkinson, op. cit., pp. 25, 37, 42.
25 Velleius Paterculus v, 4, 6–8; cf. A. J. Woodman, *Rhetoric in Classical Historiography: Four Studies* (1988), p. 116.
26 SU, p. 244; F. Millar, *A Study of Cassius Dio* (1964), p. 53 n. 1.
27 SU, p. 248f. Arrian admired Herodotus, AM, p. 134.
28 F. Millar, op. cit., pp. 7f.
29 Ibid, p. 81. For Dio on the Augustan age see J. W. Rich, in AC, pp. 86–110; on the Julio-Claudians, J. W. Humphrey, *Ancient History Bulletin*, 7, 3–4, July-Dec. 1993, pp. 148ff.
30 R. Syme, *The Roman Revolution* (1960 edn), p. 488.
31 MC, p. 9.
32 CWF, pp. 89f, RS/*T*, pp. 365, 398.
33 Dio, LIII.19 (tr. I. Scott-Kilvert).
34 Ibid, LXI.8.8; cf. PP, p. 155 n. 19.
35 Dio, LXII.18.3–4; cf. MC, p. 9.
36 F. Millar, op. cit., p. 53.
37 G. T. Griffith, in MP, 1968, p. 298.

38 SU, p. 251.
39 F. Millar, op. cit., p. 174.
40 R. Syme, *Ammianus and the Historia Augusta* (1968), *Emperors and Biography: Studies in the Historia Augusta* (1971), RS/*FH*, pp. 4f ('a literary hoax?'), AM, Ch. 9 (pp. 143–80).
41 Ibid, p. 53; R. Macpherson, *Rome in Involution: Cassiodorus's 'Variae' in their Literary and Historical Setting* (1989).

Lost Historians

1 G. T. Griffith, in MP, p. 184. For the *logographoi* see Pauly-Wissowa, *Realencyclopädie*, XIII, 1, 1021–7.
2 Hecataeus, fragment 1.
3 JBB, p. 62. Herodotus derived his concern for geography from Hecataeus, AM, p. 211.
4 JBB, p. 17.
5 F. W. Walbank, in TAD/*LH*, p. 48.
6 Cicero, *On the Orator*, II, 12.5; JBB, pp. 30ff, 105.
7 AM, p. 132, RS/*FH*, p. 3, MG/*AH*, p. 127. He was 'nearly mythical', according to Photius.
8 JBB, pp. 267f.
9 Polybius, XII, pp. 25f n. 1.
10 CWF, p. 145, MC, p. 12.
11 JBB, p. 164, SU, p. 101; cf. p. 108.
12 Strabo, VII, 3.9; cf. MG/*AH*, p. 138.
13 SU, p. 102, F. W. Walbank, in TAD/*LH*, p. 47.
14 Strabo, IX, 3.11f, C.422f. Ephorus did not ignore geography, but treated it as introductory or secondary, AM, p. 215.
15 CWF, p. 44, JBB, loc. cit.
16 SU, loc. cit.
17 A. Momigliano, in MIF/*LGNA*, pp. 167f.
18 SU, p. 101, PGW, p. 71; cf. D. A. Russell, *Plutarch* (1973), pp. 104f.
19 MG/*AH*, p. 139 and n. 19.
20 MC, p. 11, CWF, p. 82.
21 M. Fox, *JRS*, LXXXIII, 1993, p. 43, JBB, p. 166 and n. 1. Cicero, *Laws*, I.1.5, also called Theopompus a liar.
22 Polybius, XII.
23 F. W. Walbank, in TAD/*LH*, p. 54; cf. JBB, pp. 168f.
24 G. L. Barber, *OCD*, p. 1074. Timaeus was the only leading historian of his time to connect himself with Herodotus, AM, pp. 216f.
25 W. D. Ross, ibid, p. 115. For their disappearance being partly due to their poor quality, A. Lesky, *A History of Greek Literature* (1966), p. 567.
26 Cicero, *Letters to His Brother Quintus*, II, 13.4; cf. CWF, pp. 145f, FWW, p. 246, PGW, pp. 2f and n. 2.
27 PGW, pp. 29f, 33, FWW, pp. 35f.
28 Polybius, II, 56. Polybius also attacked Antisthenes of Rhodes for anti-Roman slanders. For Diocles of Peparethos see below, n. 38.

29 JBB, p. 196.
30 There were 52 books of his *Histories*.
31 And Posidonius was a great admirer of Pompey the Great.
32 P. Treves, *OCD*, pp. 867f.
33 J. Griffin, in K. J. Dover (ed.) *Ancient Greek Literature* (1980), p. 152. But M. I. Finley thought that Posidonius's contribution to the philosophy of history was negligible, MIF/*UAH*, p. 12, n.
34 A. Momigliano, in MIF/*LGNA*, p. 173.
35 P. E. Easterling and B. M. W. Knox, *The Cambridge History of Classical Literature*, 1985, p. 633.
36 F. W. Walbank, *OCD*, p. 42.
37 A. Momigliano, op. cit., p. 171.
38 A. H. McDonald, *OCD*, p. 4. E.g. Fabius Pictor relied on a Greek, Diocles of Peparethos, for the foundation of Rome.
39 Polybius, I, 14, 2–3; cf. F. W. Walbank, in TAD/*LH*, p. 40, SU, p. 131, MG/*AH*, p. 143, JBB, pp. 197f.
40 SU, p. 131.
41 E. Badian, in TAD/*LH*, pp. 2, 6, F. W. Walbank, ibid, p. 39.
42 Gellius, II, 18.2, Polybius, XXXIX, 1, F. W. Walbank, op. cit., p. 45. Cicero attacked Clitarchus and Stratocles for inventing the suicide of Themistocles.
43 E. Badian, op. cit., pp. 7, 9, R. Syme, *HHA*, p. 188, MC, p. 7, MG/*AH*, pp. 170f.
44 A. H. McDonald, *OCD*, p. 65, E. Badian, op. cit., p. 15.
45 E. Badian, op. cit., p. 12.
46 Ibid, p. 14.
47 PGW, p. 29, RMe, p. 18.
48 E. Badian, op. cit., pp. 15–17, P. G. Walsh, ibid, p. 122, RMa, p. 17.
49 E. Badian, op. cit., p. 23.
50 Ibid, pp. 24f.
51 Ibid, pp. 21, 35 n. 108, 36 n. 110, R. M. Ogilvie, *A Commentary on Livy: Books 1–5* (1965), pp. 14f, PGW, p. 122.
52 E. Badian, op. cit., p. 21 and n. 107.
53 Livy, XXVI, 49.3, XXXIII, 10.8, XXXVI, 38.6.
54 A. H. McDonald, *OCD*, p. 1106, JBB, pp. 227 n. 1.
55 E. Badian, op. cit., pp. 19, 21.
56 CWF, p. 70; Sallust, *Jugurtha*, 95.2, criticises his pro-Sullan bias.
57 P. G. Walsh, in TAD/*LH*, p. 176 n. 58, R. M. Ogilvie, op. cit., p. 8.
58 P. J. Enk, *OCD*, pp. 1107f.
59 A. H. McDonald, ibid, pp. 852f, R. Syme, *HHA*, p. 197, RS/*T*, II, p. 573.
60 *Scriptores Historiae Augustae, Aurelian*, II, 1 (tr. D. Magie).
61 See JP, pp. 1–3, on the New Testament's interest in truth. Cf. A. Cameron, in AC, pp. 5ff.
62 A. H. McDonald, op. cit., pp. 1096f, R. Syme, RS/*T*, I, p. 528 (cf. Justin, XXXVIII, 4.7), FWW, p. 242.
63 H. Chadwick, *The Early Church* (1967), pp. 102f; cf. A. H. M. Jones, *OCD*, p. 23.
64 H. Chadwick, op. cit., p. 117; HEB, p. 46; cf. p. 52.

Information from Other Sources

1 MC, p. ix.
2 A. Toynbee, *The Legacy of Greece* (1921), p. 300.
3 E. Gabba, MC, pp. 55, 58.
4 A. Snodgrass, ibid, pp. 137, 139. As a result of this 'historians are now emancipated from historiography', K. J. Dover, *History and Theory*, XXII, 1983, p. 59.
5 M. Grant, *The Visible Past* (1990), pp. xvf, AM, p. 136, MIF/*UAH*, pp. 87–101 ('Archaeology and History'). On the artistic aspects, F. Haskell, *History and its Images: Art and the Interpretation of the Past* (1993).
6 F. Millar, in MC, pp. 80f; cf. B. F. Cook, *Greek Inscriptions* (1987, 1990), L. Keppie, *Understanding Roman Inscriptions* (1992). Inscriptions correct Polybius on Boeotia and Aetolia (p. 71 above). Mommsen was the first Roman historian to use inscriptions systematically, AM, loc. cit.
7 F. Millar, op. cit., pp. 81f.
8 A. Lesky, *A History of Greek Literature* (1966), pp. 5f.
9 G. L. Barber, *OCD*, p. 766.
10 G. T. Griffith, in MP, pp. 192, 194; cf. p. 232.
11 Ibid, pp. 194f; P. Levi, *A History of Greek Literature* (1985), p. 404.
12 M. Crawford, in MC, p. 187; cf. M. Grant, *Roman History From Coins* (1958, 1968). Mommsen began to make good use of coins, AM, p. 136.
13 J. Kent, in J. Wacher (ed.) *The Roman World*, II, 1987, p. 568.
14 E. Gabba, *JRS*, LXXXI, 1981, p. 50.

Misinformation from Other Sources

1 M. Grant, *The Roman Forum* (1970), p. 84. Cf. G. C. Le Gendre, *Traité de l'opinion ou mémoires pour servir a l'histoire de l'esprit humain* (1735): 'le marbre et l'airain mentent quelquefois'.
2 M. Grant, *The Emperor Constantine* (1993), p. 204.
3 R. Brilliant, *Roman Art* (1974), p. 175, fig. IV.13. Cf. an idealised statue of Augustus in the Louvre, F. A. Abbate, *Roman Art* (1972), pp. 1, 26, etc., and Claudius (p. 124).
4 J. B. Bury and R. Meiggs, *A History of Greece* (4th edn, 1975), pp. 529f.
5 F. E. Adcock, *Cambridge Ancient History*, X, 1934, p. 593: 'truth is not all its purpose.'
6 E.g. M. Crawford, *Roman Republican Coinage* (1974), pp. 352 no. 344, 414 no. 404 (Tatius), p. 451 no. 477.2 (Romulus Quirinus), etc.
7 H. Mattingly, *A Catalogue of the Roman Coins in the British Museum*, I, 1928, no. 1.
8 Ibid, V, 1950, pp. 41, 136, 140f, 143.
9 A. R. Birley, *Marcus Aurelius* (1987), pp. 184, 198f; cf. the honouring of Septimius Severus as the brother of the (now deified, formerly vilified) Commodus, *Corpus Inscriptionum Latinarum*, VI, 1365, 1577.

10 H. Mattingly, op. cit., III, 1936, pp. lxxxvi, 124 (Hadriano Traiano Caesari).
11 B. W. Henderson, *The Life and Principate of the Emperor Hadrian* (1923), p. 35 (cf. p. 38); M. Cary and H. H. Scullard, *A History of Rome* (3rd edn, 1975), p. 642 n. 5; cf. C. M. Wells, *The Roman Empire* (2nd edn, 1992), p. 202. (But, Henderson concludes, Trajan undoubtedly intended Hadrian to succeed him: there was no other possible candidate, and any other solution would have provoked civil war.)
12 P. Levi, *A History of Greek Literature* (1985), p. 404.
13 G. T. Griffith, in MP, p. 195.
14 A. Lesky, *A History of Greek Literature* (1966), p. 567.

CONCLUSION

1 Cf. *Times Literary Supplement* 16/3/92, p. 12.

BIBLIOGRAPHY

ANCIENT WRITERS

Greek writers

Aeschylus, of Eleusis, 525/524–456 BC. Athenian tragic dramatist.

Africanus, see Julius Africanus.

Albinus, Aulus Postumius, 2nd century BC. Consul, historian and poet. See pp. 107–118 (in which other lost historians in this list are also discussed).

Alexander Polyhistor, of Miletus, *c.* 105 to after 40 BC. Writer on many subjects.

Antiochus, of Syracuse, 5th century BC. Historian of Sicily and Italy.

Antisthenes, of Rhodes, early 2nd century BC. Philosopher and historian.

Appian, of Alexandria, late 1st and early 2nd century AD. Historian. See p. 104.

Aratus, of Sicyon, 271–213 BC. Statesman and autobiographer.

Archilochus, of Paros, *c.* 710 to after 648 BC (?). Poet.

Aristides, Aelius, of Mysia, AD 117 or 129–181 or later. Writer on many subjects and lecturer.

Aristophanes, of Athens, 457/445 to before 385 BC. Comic dramatist (Old Comedy).

Aristotle, of Stagirus, 384–322 BC. Philosopher and scientist. His historical study, the *Constitution of Athens* (*Athenaion Politeia*), has survived: see p. 121.

Arrian, of Bithynia, 2nd century AD. Historian. See p. 104.

Athenaion Politeia, see *Constitution of Athens²*.

Callisthenes, of Olynthus, d. 327 BC. Historian.

Chaereas, later 3rd century BC. Historian of the Second Punic War.

Clitarchus, of Alexandria, early 3rd century BC. Historian.

Constitution of Athens (1) (The Old Oligarch), 5th century BC. Wrongly attributed to Xenophon. See p. 100.

Constitution of Athens (2) (*Athenaion Politeia*). See Aristotle.

Ctesias, of Cnidus, late 5th century BC. Doctor and historian.

Dio Cassius, of Nicaea, *c.* AD 155–235. Historian. See p. 104.

156

Diocles, of Peparethos, 3rd century BC. Historian of Rome.

Diodorus Siculus, of Agyrium, later 1st century BC. Historian. See p. 101.

Dionysius, of Halicarnassus, later 1st century BC. Rhetor and historian. See p. 101.

Duris, of Samos, c. 340–c. 260 BC. 'Tyrant', historian and critic.

Ephorus, of Cyme, c. 405–330 BC. Historian.

Epictetus, of Hierapolis (Phrygia), c. AD 55–c. 135. Stoic philosopher.

Eratosthenes, of Cyrene, c. 275–194 BC. Mathematician and geographer.

Euripides, of Phyla, c. 485/480–c. 406 BC. Athenian tragic dramatist.

Eusebius, of Caesarea Maritima, c. AD 260–340. Christian historian.

Fabius Pictor, Quintus, see Pictor.

Gorgias, of Leontini, c. 483–376 BC. Sophist (teacher of rhetoric).

Hecataeus, of Miletus, c. 500 BC. Geographer and historian.

Hellanicus, of Lesbos, 5th century BC. Historian.

Heraclitus, of Ephesus, c. 500 BC. Philosopher.

Herodotus, of Halicarnassus, 5th century BC. Historian. See pp. 5–7 and *passim*.

Hesiod, of Cyme, 8th Century BC. Epic poet. See p. 25.

Homer, of Chios, 8th century BC. Epic poet. See p. 25.

Isocrates, of Athens, 436–338 BC. Rhetorician, educationalist and political theorist.

Josephus, of Jerusalem, AD 37/38 to 94/95. Historian of the Jews. See p. 17 and *passim*.

Julius Africanus, Sextus, of Jerusalem (Aelia Capitolina), early 3rd century AD. Christian traveller, librarian and historian, etc.

Lucian, of Samosata, born c. AD 120. Writer on Herodotus and many other subjects.

Marcellinus, 6th century AD. Biographer of Thucydides.

Old Oligarch, The. See *Constitution of Athens* (1).

Oxyrhynchus Historian, The, early 4th century BC. See p. 120–1.

Panyassis, of Halicarnassus, 5th century BC. Epic poet.

Photius, 9th century AD. Patriarch of Constantinople and scholar and lexicographer.

Phylarchus, of Athens, late 3rd century BC. Historian.

Pictor, Quintus Fabius, later 3rd century BC. Senator and historian.

Plato, of Athens, c. 429–347 BC. Philosopher.

Plutarch, of Chaeronea, before AD 50 to after 120. Biographer, etc. See pp. 18–20 and *passim*.

Polybius, of Megalopolis, c. 200 to after 118 BC. Historian. See pp. 10–13 and *passim*.

Porphyry, of Tyre (or Batanea), AD 232/3–c. 305. Scholar, philosopher , pagan student of religion.

Posidonius, of Apamea (on the River Orontes), c. 135–c. 51/50 BC. Historian and polymath.

Pseudo-Xenophon. See *Constitution of Athens* (1).

Solon, of Athens, early 6th century BC. Statesman and poet.

Sophocles, of Colonus, c. 496–406 BC. Athenian tragic dramatist.

Sosylus, of Sparta, later 3rd century BC. Historian of the Second Punic War.

Stesichorus, of Mataurus, *c.* 632/629–*c.* 556/553 BC (?). Lyric poet.
Strabo, of Amasia, *c.* 63 BC to at least AD 21. Geographer and historian.
Stratocles, of Rhodes, *c.* 100 BC. Stoic historian and biographer.
Theagenes, of Rhegium, later 6th century BC. Allegorical interpreter of Homer.
Theopompus, of Chios, 4th century BC. Historian.
Thucydides, of Athens, *c.* 460/455–*c.* 400 BC. Historian. See pp. 7–9 and *passim.*
Timaeus, of Tauromenium, *c.* 356–260 BC. Historian.
Xenophanes, of Colophon, 6th and 5th centuries BC. Poet and philosopher.
Xenophon, of Erchia, *c.* 428–*c.* 354 BC. Soldier, man of letters, historian. See p. 9 and *passim.*

Latin writers

Aemilius Scaurus, Marcus, see Scaurus.
Agrippina the Younger, AD 15–59. Empress and biographer.
Ammianus Marcellinus, of Antioch, *c.* AD 330–395. Historian. See p. 23 and *passim.*
Annales Maximi, in 80 books. Published in later 2nd century BC. Official records of events.
Antias, Valerius, of Antium, 1st century BC. Historian.
Antipater, Lucius Coelius, late 2nd century BC. Jurist, rhetorician, historian.
Antonius, Marcus, consul 99, censor 97 BC. Orator, author of a rhetorical treatise.
Asellio, Sempronius, 2nd century BC. Historian.
Asinius Pollio, Gaius, see Pollio.
Caesar, Gaius Julius, 100–44 BC. Dictator, writer of *Commentaries*. See p. 13 and *passim.*
Cassiodorus, of Scylacium, *c.* AD 490–583. Statesman, historian, etc.
Cato the Elder, Marcus Porcius (the Censor), of Tusculum, 234–149 BC. Statesman, agriculturalist, historian.
Cicero, Marcus Tullius, of Arpinum, 100–43 BC. Orator, writer on oratory, philosophy, history, etc., letter-writer, statesman.
Claudius Quadrigarius, Quintus, see Quadrigarius.
Coelius Antipater, Lucius, see Antipater.
Cornelius, see Nepos, Sisenna, Sulla, Tacitus.
Curtius Rufus, Quintus, see Rufus.
Fabius Quintilianus, Marcus, see Quintilian.
Fannius, Gaius. Consul 122 BC. Historian.
Gellius, Cnaeus. Later 2nd century BC. Historian.
Gracchus, Gaius Sempronius, 153–121 BC. Politician and biographer.
Hieronymus, Eusebius, see Jerome.
Hirtius, Aulus. Consul 43 BC. Historian, propgandist and letter-writer.
Historia Augusta, see *Scriptores Historiae Augustae.*
Horace (Quintus Horatius Flaccus), of Venusia, 65–8 BC. Poet.

Jerome, St (Eusebius Hieronymus), of Stridon (on border of Dalmatia and Pannonia), *c.* AD 340–420. Theologian.

Julius Caesar, Gaius, see Caesar.

Justin (Marcus Junianus Justinus), 3rd century BC. Epitomator of Trogus.

Licinius Macer, Gaius, see Macer.

Livy (Titus Livius), of Patavium, 64/59 BC-AD 12/17. Historian. See p. 16 and *passim.*

Macer, Gaius Licinius, praetor 68 BC. Historian.

Macrobius, Ambrosius Theodosius, from Africa (?), late 4th and early 5th centuries AD. Neoplatonist and miscellaneous writer.

Nepos, Cornelius, of Cisalpine Gaul, *c.* 99–*c.* 24 BC. Biographer. See Chapter 20.

Orosius, Paulus, of Spain, 5th century AD. Christian historian.

Paterculus, Velleius, see Velleius.

Pliny the Elder (Gaius Plinius Secondus), AD 23/24–79. Officer and writer on Natural History and many other subjects.

Pliny the Younger (Gaius Plinius Caecilius Secundus), *c.* AD 61–*c.* 112. Letter-writer and poet.

Pollio, Gaius Asinius. 76 BC-AD 4; consul 40 BC. Historian, poet, orator.

Pompeius, Trogus, see Trogus.

Quadrigarius, Quintus Claudius, early 1st century BC. Historian.

Quintilian (Marcus Fabius Quintilianus), of Calagurris, *c.* AD 30/35–100. Rhetorician and literary critic.

Rufus, Quintus Curtius, mid-1st century AD (?). Rhetorician and historian.

Rufus, Publius Rutilius, consul 105 BC. Historian.

Sallust, (Gaius Sallustius Crispus), *c.* 86–35 BC. Praetor and historian. See pp. 14–16 and *passim.*

Scaurus, Marcus Aemilius, consul 115 BC. Autobiographer.

Scriptores Historiae Augustae (writers of the *Historia Augusta*, fictitiously named), probably 4th century AD. Biographers.

Sempronius Asellio, see Asellio.

Seneca the Elder (Lucius Annaeus Seneca), of Corduba, born *c.* 55 BC. Writer on rhetoric.

Seneca the Younger (Lucius Annaeus Seneca), of Corduba, 4 BC/AD 1 to 65. Statesman, philosopher, tragic dramatist, letter-writer.

Sisenna, Lucius Cornelius, praetor 78 BC. Historian and translator.

Suetonius (Gaius Suetonius Tranquillus), of Hippo Regius, *c.* AD 69 to after 121/122. Biographer. See pp. 21–3 and *passim.*

Sulla, Lucius Cornelius, *c.* 138–78 BC. Dictator and autobiographer.

Tacitus, Cornelius, of Gaul (German frontier?) or Cisalpine Gaul (north Italy), *c.* AD 36–*c.* 116. Historian, biographer and writer on oratory. See p. 20 and *passim.*

Terentius Varro, Marcus, see Varro.

Tertullian (Quintus Septimius Florens Tertullianus), of Carthage (or nearby), *c.* AD 160–*c.* 240. Christian theologian.

Trogus, Pompeius, of Narbonese Gaul (a Vocontian), late 1st century BC. Historian and scientist.

Tullius Cicero, Marcus, see Cicero.

Varro, Marcus Terentius, of Reate, 116–27 BC. Historian, biographer, geographer, agriculturalist, philosophical satirist.
Velleius Paterculus, of Campanian descent, c. 19 BC to after AD 30. Officer and historian. See p. 103.
Virgil (Publius Vergilius Maro), of Andes (Mantua), 70–19 BC. Poet.

Modern Writers

Adcock, F. E. (1956) *Caesar as Man of Letters*, Cambridge: Cambridge University Press.
Anderson, J. K. (1974) *Xenophon*, London: Duckworth.
Appleby, J. (1994) *Telling the Truth about History*, New York: Norton.
Baldwin, B. (1983) *Suetonius*, Benjamin's North Americana.
Baldwin, P. (ed.) (1990) *Reworking the Past*, Boston: Beacon Press.
Barnes, H. E. (1937) *A History of Historical Writing*, University of Oklahoma (reprinted 1962, New York: Dover).
Barrow, R. H. (1967) *Plutarch and His Times*, London: Chatto & Windus.
Brunt, P. A. (1993) *Studies in Greek History and Thought*, Oxford: Oxford University Press.
Burnham, T. (1980) *More Misinformation*, New York: Lippincroft & Crowell.
Bury, J. B. (1908) *Ancient Greek Historians*, New York: Dover (reprinted 1958).
Cameron, A. (ed.) (1989) *History as Text: The Writing of Ancient History*, London: Duckworth.
Cartledge, P. (1993) *The Greeks: A Portrait of Self and Others*, Oxford: Oxford University Press.
Clarke, M. L. (1953) *Rhetoric at Rome*, London: Cohen & West.
Collingwood, R. G. (1946) *The Idea of History*, Oxford: Clarendon Press, (revised edn [with lectures 1926–8] 1993).
Collingwood, R. G. (1966) *Essays in the Philosophy of History*, New York: McGraw Hill.
Conley, T. M. (1994) *Rhetoric in the European Tradition*, Oxford: Blackwell.
Connor, W. R. (1984) *Thucydides*, Princeton University Press (reprinted 1987).
Cornford, F. M. (1907) *Thucydides Mythistoricus*, London: E. Arnold (reprinted 1965, London: Routledge & Kegan Paul).
Crawford, M. (ed.) (1983) *Sources for Ancient History*, Cambridge: Cambridge University Press.
Crum, R. H. (1991) *Rethinking History: The War Myth from Pericles to Roosevelt: With Other Historical Studies*, Cornwall, Ontario: Vesta.
Dance, E. H. (1960) *History the Betrayer: A Study of Bias*, London: Hutchinson (reprinted 1964).
Danto, A. C. (1968) *Analytical Philosophy of History*, Cambridge: Cambridge University Press.
Detienne, M. and Vernant, J.-P. (1991) *Cunning Intelligence in Greek Culture and Society*, University of Chicago.

Dorey, T. A. (ed.) (1966) *Latin Historians*, London: Routledge & Kegan Paul.

Dorey, T. A. (ed.) (1967) *Latin Biography*, London: Routledge & Kegan Paul.

Dorey, T. A. (ed.) (1969) *Tacitus*, London: Routledge & Kegan Paul.

Dorey, T. A. (ed.) (1971) *Livy*, London: Routledge & Kegan Paul.

Dover, K. J. (1973) *Thucydides*, Oxford: Clarendon Press.

Dover, K. J. (ed.) (1980) *Ancient Greek Literature*, Oxford: Oxford University Press.

Dudley, D. R. (1968) *The World of Tacitus*, London: Secker & Warburg.

Eadie, J. W. and Ober, J. (eds) (1985) *The Craft of the Ancient Historian* (Essays in Honor of C. G. Starr), Lanham.

Evans, J. A. S. (1982) *Herodotus*, Boston: Twayne.

Evans, J. A. S. (1991) *Herodotus: Explorer of the Past*, Princeton University Press.

Evans, J. de R. (1992) *The Art of Persuasion: Political Propaganda from Aeneas to Brutus*, University of Michigan Press.

Fehling, D. (1989) *Herodotus and his 'Sources'*, Leeds.

Finberg, H. P. R. (ed.) (1962) *Approaches to History*, London: Routledge & Kegan Paul (reprinted 1965).

Finley, J. H. (1967) *Three Essays on Thucydides*, Harvard University Press.

Finley, M. I. (1971) *The Use and Abuse of History*, Harmondsworth: Penguin.

Finley, M. I. (1973) *The Ancient Economy*, London: Chatto & Windus, (2nd edn 1985, London: Hogarth Press).

Finley, M. I. (1985) *Ancient History*, London: Chatto & Windus.

Finley, M. I. (ed.) (1959) *The Greek Historians*, London: Chatto & Windus.

Finley, M. I. (ed.) (1981) *The Legacy of Greece: A New Appraisal*, Oxford: Oxford University Press.

Fornara, C. W. (1983) *The Nature of History in Ancient Greece and Rome*, University of California, Berkeley and Los Angeles.

Gallie, W. B. (1964) *Philosophy and the Historical Understanding*, London: Chatto & Windus.

Gardiner, P. (ed.) (1959) *Theories of History*, New York: Free Press.

Garraty, J. A. (1957) *The Nature of Biography*, New York: Knopf.

Gay, P. (1974) *Style in History*, London: Norton.

Geyl, P. (1962) *Debates with Historians*, London: Fontana (Collins).

Gill, C. and Wiseman, T. P. (eds) (1993) *Lies and Fiction in the Ancient World*, University of Exeter.

Goodyear, F. R. D. (1970) *Tacitus*, Oxford: Clarendon Press.

Gould, J. (1989) *Herodotus*, London: St Martin's.

Grant, M. (1952) *Ancient History*, London: Methuen.

Grant, M. (1969) *Julius Caesar*, London: Weidenfeld & Nicolson (reprinted 1992).

Grant, M. (1970) *The Ancient Historians*, London: Weidenfeld & Nicolson.

Grant, M. (1992) *Readings in the Classical Historians*, New York: Scribner's.

Hadas, M. (1950) *A History of Greek Literature*, New York: Columbia University Press.

Hadas, M. (1952) *A History of Latin Literature*, New York: Columbia University Press.

Hadas-Lebel, M. (1993) *Flavius Josephus*, New York: Macmillan.

Hall, E. (1991) *Inventing the Barbarian; Greek Self-Definition Through Tragedy*, Oxford: Oxford University Press.

Harrison, F. (1894) *The Meaning of History, etc.*, London: Macmillan.

Hart, J. (1982) *Herodotus and Greek History*, London: Croom Helm.

Haskell, F. (1993) *History and Its Images: Art and the Interpretation of the Past*, Yale University Press.

Henry, W. P. (1966) *Greek Historical Writing: A Historiographical Essay based on Xenophon's Hellenica*, Chicago: Argonaut.

Hexter, J. B. (1961) *Reappraisals in History*, London: Longman.

Histoire et Historiens dans l'Antiquité (Fondation Hardt), Entretiens sur l'Antiquité Classique, IV), Geneva: Vandoeuvres, 1956.

Hornblower, S. (1987) *Thucydides*, London: Duckworth.

Hunter, V. J. (1982) *Past and Process in Herodotus and Thucydides*, Princeton University Press.

Hunter, V. J. (1993) *Thucydides the Artful Reporter*, Toronto.

Jenkins, K. (1992) *Rethinking History*, London: Routledge.

Jones, C. P. (1971) *Plutarch and Rome*, Oxford: Clarendon Press.

Jones, T. B. (1967) *Paths to the Ancient Past*, New York: Free Press.

Kagan, D. (1975) *Studies in the Greek Historians*, Cambridge: Cambridge University Press.

Kennedy, G. (1963) *The Art of Persuasion in Greece*, London: Routledge & Kegan Paul.

Kennedy, G. (1972) *The Art of Rhetoric in the Roman World*, Princeton University Press.

Lateiner, D. (1989) *The Historical Method of Herodotus*, Toronto.

Lesky, A. (1966) *A History of Greek Literature*, London: Methuen.

Levi, P. (1985) *A History of Greek Literature*, Harmondsworth: Penguin (Viking).

Lloyd, C. (1993) *The Structure of History*, Oxford: Blackwell.

Lloyd-Jones, H. (1971) *The Justice of Zeus*, University of California Press, Berkeley and Los Angeles.

Lounsbury, R. C. (1987) *The Art of Suetonius: An Introduction*, P. Lang.

MacQueen, B. D. (1990) *Myth, Rhetoric and Fiction*, University of Nebraska Press.

Martin, R. (1981) *Tacitus*, London: Batsford.

Marwick, A. (1988) *Beauty in History*, London: Thames & Hudson.

Mayer, C. S. (1988) *The Unmasterable Past*, Harvard University Press.

Mellor, R. (1993) *Tacitus*, New York: Routledge.

Meyerhoff, H. (ed.) (1959) *The Philosophy of History in Our Time*, New York: Doubleday.

Momigliano, A. (1966) *Studies in Historiography*, New York: Harper & Row.

Momigliano, A. (1971, 1993) *The Development of Greek Biography*, Harvard University Press.

Muller, H. J. (1952) *The Uses of the Past*, New York: Mentor (NAL).
Myers, J. L. (1953) *Herodotus: Father of History*, Oxford: Clarendon Press.
Nickel, R. (1959) *Xenophon*, Darmstadt.
Percival, J. (1991) *Truth in the Greek and Roman Historians* (ARLT Summer School), Cardiff.
Perkin, H. (ed.) (1970) *History*, London: Routledge & Kegan Paul.
Plass, P. (1988) *Wit and the Writing of History: The Rhetoric of Historiography in Imperial Rome*, Wisconsin University Press.
Platnauer, M. (ed.) (1968) *Fifty Years (and Twelve) of Classical Scholarship*.
Porter, H. (1984) *Lies, Damned Lies and Some Exclusives*, London: Chatto & Windus.
Pritchett, W. K. (1993) *The Liar School of Herodotus*, Gieben, Netherlands.
Rajak, T. (1983) *Josephus: The Historian and His Society*, London: Duckworth.
Renier, G. J. (1950) *History: Its Purpose and Method*, Mercer University Press (Rose), Macon (reprinted 1982).
Riffaterre, M. (1990) *Fictional Truth*, Baltimore University Press.
Rogers, C. L. (1992) *The Topical Josephus*.
Romilly, J. de (1985) *A Short History of Greek Literature*, Chicago University Press.
Russell, D. A. (1973) *Plutarch*, London: Duckworth.
Sacks, K. (1981) *Polybius on the Writing of History*, University of California Press, Berkeley and Los Angeles.
Scanlon, T. F. (1987) *Spes Frustrata: A Reading of Sallust*, Heidelberg: Winter.
Seager, R. (1986) *Ammianus Marcellinus; Seven Studies in His Language and Thought*, University of Missouri Press.
Shenkman, R. (1993) *Legends, Lies and Cherished Myths of World History*, New York: Harper-Collins.
Sordi, M. (ed.) (1975) *Storiographia e Propaganda*, Università Cattolica del Sacro Cuore, Milan.
Stadter, P. A. (ed.) (1992) *Plutarch and the Historical Tradition*, London; Routledge.
Syme, R. (1958) *Tacitus*, Oxford: Clarendon Press.
Syme, R. (1964) *Sallust*, University of California Press, Berkeley and Los Angeles.
Syme, R. (1970) *Ten Studies in Tacitus*, Oxford: Clarendon Press.
Syme, R. (1984) *Fictional History Old and New: Hadrian* (lecture), Somerville College, Oxford.
Teggart, F. J. (1972) *Theory and Processes of History*, Gloucester, Massachusetts: Peter Smith.
The Greek Historians: Literature and History (papers presented to A. E. Raubitschek), Stanford University, California, 1985.
Thomas, G. (ed.) (1990) *The Unresolved Past*, London: Weidenfeld & Nicolson.
Thomas, R. (1989) *Oral Tradition and Written Record in Classical Athens*, Cambridge: Cambridge University Press.

Tulloch, H. (1988) *Acton*, London: Weidenfeld & Nicolson.

Usher, S. (1969) *The Historians of Greece and Rome*, London: Hamish Hamilton.

Veyne, P. (1984) *Writing History: Essay on Epistemology*, Middletown, Connecticut: Wesleyan Union Press.

Walbank, F. W. (1965) *Speeches in Greek Historians*, Oxford: Oxford University Press.

Walbank, F. W. (1972) *Polybius*, University of California Press, Berkeley and Los Angeles (reprinted 1990).

Walker, B. (1952) *The Annals of Tacitus*, Manchester University Press.

Wallace-Hadrill, A. (1983) *Suetonius: The Scholar and His Caesars*, London: Duckworth.

Walsh, P. G. (1967) *Livy: His Historical Aims and Methods*, Cambridge: Cambridge University Press.

Walsh, P. G. (1974) *Livy*, Oxford: Clarendon Press.

Waters, K. H. (1984) *Herodotus the Historian*, London: Croom Helm.

Westlake, H. D. (1968) *Individuals in Thucydides*, Cambridge: Cambridge University Press.

Westlake, H. D. (1969) *Essays on the Greek Historians and Greek History*, Manchester: Manchester University Press and New York: Barnes & Noble.

Winks, R. W. (ed.) (1969) *The Historian as Detective: Essays on Evidence*, New York: Harper & Row.

Woodman, A. J. (1988) *Rhetoric in Classical Historiography: Four Studies*, London: Croom Helm.

Yavetz, Z. (1953) *Julius Caesar and His Public Image*, Cornell University Press.

Zecchini, G. (1993) *Ricerche di storiografia latina tardo-antica*, Centro Ricerche e Documentazione sull'Antichità Classica, Rome.

INDEX

Note: The names of the twelve principal historians and biographers are omitted, because the book is all about them.